MW00565556

Unleashing Your Soul-Level Magic

Tales of Transition to Help Unwrap Your Special Gifts

Contributors:

Kim Adley, Samantha Bauer, Elizabeth Craig,

Sue Fattibene, Kelly Frost, Denise Ann Galloni,

Priscilla Green, Darlene Barruso Kruth, Amanda Kunkel,

Marta Mazzoni, Racquelle Pakutz, and Maryann Udel

Stories Collected by Cori Wamsley

Aurora Corialis Publishing

Pittsburgh, PA

Unleashing Your Soul-Level Magic: Tales of Transition to Help Unwrap Your Special Gifts

For more information, please contact cori@coriwamsley.com.

Inspiring quote by Muriel Rukeyser from the poem "The Speed of Darkness," *The Speed of Darkness* (Random House, 1968).

Paperback ISBN: 978-1-958481-82-0

Ebook ISBN: 978-1-958481-83-7

Printed in the United States of America

Cover by Karen Captline, BetterBe Creative

Edited by Renee Picard, Aurora Corialis Publishing

Advance Praise

"Every woman, including the women in this book, faces immeasurable struggles, and incredulous come backs, which are quite often hidden behind the four walls of their home. It is still suggested that women sit still and look pretty, and any woman who defies this suggestion is considered a nuisance, but little by little, women are gaining confidence, strength, and most importantly their voice. The voice of one woman who shares their struggles, their embarrassments and triumphs, has the power to inspire thousands of other women who were afraid they were alone in the same battles.

"The brave women of *Unleashing Your Soul-Level Magic* are sharing their voices, and empowering women everywhere. This is a book that you'll want to read again and again as you develop your own voice, which you will find as the very stepping-stone to overcoming your own personal struggles."

~ Mandi Pryor

MP Marketing and PR: The Jumpstart Factory

mpmarketingandpr.com

"*Unleashing Your Soul-Level Magic* is an inspirational book. It's a collection of moving stories by talented women authors who share their secrets to unleashing magical outcomes through passion, compassion, and inventiveness.

"One poignant example: Darlene Barruso Kruth, in "Creating and Embracing my Dear Friend's Legacy," tells the jarring story of losing her best friend, Tom, while attending Duquesne University in the 1980s. Tom's unexpected death triggered a search for purpose, ultimately leading the author to discover her gift for stewarding scholarship initiatives for others.

"This book is a refreshing antidote to the often disturbing and depressing stories that pervade our societal discourse today. It's certain to unleash magic for everyone."

~ Ken Gormley

President of Duquesne University, Award-Winning Author

"*Unleashing Your Soul-Level Magic* is an anthology that will stir your empathy and help you see that you are not alone in your journey. The women's impactful stories will leave you encouraged to create your own magic, in your unique and beautiful way as they have. I have been positively affected by these women's tales. This is a must-read book for women in transition who desire reflection and heart-centered reading."

~ Dr. Shellie Hipsky

CEO of Inspiring Lives International, Executive Director of the Global Sisterhood, Editor-in-Chief of *Inspiring Lives Magazine*, 15-Time Bestselling Author, and The Global Empowerment Coach

shelliehipsky.com

"The sharing of our individual stories is truly an act of bravery. By sharing our truth we are able to connect deeply with others, and see the light at the end of our own tunnel. The exemplary stories in this anthology certainly live up to the definition of bravery, connection, and inspiration."

~Connie Capiotis

CEO of Full Flavor Leadership, Executive Director of Digital Bridges Pittsburgh

fullflavorleadership.com

digitalbridgespgh.org

"*Kelly in Paris* should be the title of a Netflix series. Especially since Kelly's story of turning fear, trepidation, and uncertainty into a personal adventure is so eloquently and boldly told in these pages. Traveling to other countries, meeting new people, eating strange foods, seeing iconic edifices, and exploring different cultures is perhaps the greatest opportunity for personal development. You can't find it in a book, on a Google search or by scrolling through your social media feed. Life is best experienced by living. Had Kelly said 'no' and let fear get the best of her, she would have missed out on an adventure that took her beyond the Eiffel Tower, The Louvre, and a famous cemetery: the adventure that happens after you conquer your fears. And that message is echoed throughout this book.

"Kelly's living her greatest dreams born out of the courage she found in Paris. She is a beautiful example of facing your fears, serving others with great compassion and loving the life you have. I'm so happy I was the 'client,' who also had the time of her life, with Kelly in Paris."

~ Darieth Chisolm

Emmy Award Winning TV Host, Filmmaker, Author, Speaker, & Life Coach

darieth.com

Table of Contents

"The Universe is made of stories, not of atoms."

~ Muriel Rukeyser

Introduction

By Cori Wamsley

We all go through multiple transitions in our lives. Often these are triggered by loss, change, accidents, or other circumstances that lead us, sometimes kicking and screaming, into the next chapter.

Having been through many of those transitions myself, I've found I had to dig deep to get through the bigger ones.

We all have our unique gifts, sometimes lying dormant, waiting to be uncovered. These often reveal our bigger purpose.

In those moments of significant difficulty, I found myself stripped to my core, with my true gifts revealed, and no choice but to use them.

It's kind of like finding yourself locked in a closet with only the items in your purse to bust out.

In my junior year of high school, when selection for the winter brass ensemble happened, I was forgotten. I happened to be practicing a baton routine in a different area, not sitting with the rest of the trumpets. When I found out I wasn't picked, I was furious and immediately responded, "I'll start my own."

I couldn't believe that came out of my mouth! My gift of leadership and organizing revealed itself that day, as I approached our band director with that suggestion. I realize that high school stories aren't usually that inspiring, but this particular event is one I've come back to repeatedly as a testament to the power vibrating just under my skin.

When I decided to divorce my first husband about a decade later, I felt lost. Things weren't working out, and I knew we would be better off without each other. Before, I felt that I always needed someone, but in the deep sadness of this relationship, I suddenly felt that I could be on my own. It was then that my gift of independence, of doing things my way and looking out for myself and my happiness, revealed itself. Though I've had a hot and cold relationship with these gifts, they have shined brightly—finally with a constant glow—throughout my entrepreneurial journey.

Which brings me to my most recent revelation. I always knew I was a writer. I dreamed of being a famous author when I was in middle school, dabbling at book writing... and coming up short. Literally. (Fourteen notebook pages don't equal a novel, FYI.) I worked as a technical and scientific writer and editor for ten years, and although I loved the type of writing I did, there was something missing. I felt like I wasn't meeting SOME goal, but I was hard-pressed to tell what it was. It felt like failure, though the position itself looked like success. It felt like desperation when there was really no reason for it. And it felt like hopelessness, as I joked that my job was a "sentence" rather than a "career."

This last one led to a slow-release period for my deepest gift to come to the surface. I felt that the Universe left me stewing in my desire to go big or go home, teetering on the edge of something brilliant and scary that I knew would be mine... but could I handle it? Often, those deepest gifts are wrapped in mysterious packaging with a too-tight bow.

We tug. We shake the box. But it says, "do not open till Christmas," right?

Yeah, it's so worth the wait to become who you were always meant to be.

These moments that led to me finding myself and embracing my own soul-gifts are why I was inspired to collect the stories for this book. I knew, after several years of being a business owner, that people have real, raw stories that never come to the surface, and those stories must be told.

Those stories are breathtaking, jaw-dropping, and inspiring, to say the least.

Have you ever watched a baking show? The ones where they show you every step of the way from mess to masterpiece? That's what I wanted to create with this book: an entire collection of stories from women who you see every day. You may see their smile and note that they have a cool career, but what REALLY got them there? How did they uncover their gifts?

That's what I set out to discover.

If you've ever been a hair's breadth away from a miracle, then you know that all it takes is a gust of wind to make it happen. The women in this book share stories of just that—that feeling when you sense something big just over the horizon, you spin through the darkness with it, and then come out a completely different person. Yet still you. It's like being pummeled by an enormous wave and then walking up the beach afterward to dry in the sun and watch the littlest fish in a tide pool. You feel something other than human.

That, my friend, is living in your purpose as your highest self.

And that's where these women are today.

If you want to feel inspired, if you want to walk the difficult paths with those who have been there before you, and you want to be more, be the most, that you possibly can be—you've come to the right place.

The stories in this book are sometimes challenging, sometimes provocative, but completely and utterly about the soul-level magic that led these women to step into their purpose.

And I'm so honored to know them all, walk with them through their writing, and share their stories.

Please enjoy the beautiful gift you are unwrapping.

And always know your keys are in your purse.

A Matter of Choices

By Kim Adley

"Life is a matter of choices, and every choice you make makes you."

~ John C. Maxwell

I have lived my life doing the "right" thing.

Doing the right thing is a GOOD thing, but sometimes it's not the BEST thing needed to unleash human potential.

When I look back at my life journey, I conjure up sepia-colored images of a bewildered little girl who lost her daddy to a ruptured aortic aneurysm without any warning at the tender age of four. My older brother was seven, and my younger brother was 18 months.

Needless to say, this was a devastating event for my family. At the time, I didn't really understand the magnitude of the loss.

I just knew that my daddy was gone, and my mother was always sad.

My memories of that time recur sporadically as blurry snapshots. I have one recollection of me on my dad's shoulders entering a bakery. I can smell the sweetness and am giggling as a white-haired lady behind the counter hands me a cookie. I can also recall a scene where I am hiding behind a living room chair, holding my breath while I wait to jump out to surprise him as he calls out, "Where is my princess?"

And that's about it for the memories of a father in my life.

The only way I knew how to grow up was with a single parent—my mom. After she emerged from her heavy shroud of grief, she managed to raise three awesome kids on her own and never remarried. To her great credit, I didn't even realize we were poor until I was in fifth grade.

I remember that moment vividly. I was standing in the lunch line at school when the girl in front of me pointed out loudly that "she gets a free lunch!" It sounded negative, so I rebuked her and said, "No I don't!" She said, "Yes you do! Your lunch ticket is red, and mine is yellow. Red is for the FREE LUNCH PEOPLE."

Ew, I thought. I didn't want to be part of the "Free Lunch People."

I went home that day and pointedly asked my mom if I got a free lunch. She looked back at me and said very matter-of-factly, "Yes, and we get free butter and government cheese and food stamps too." It was a poignant moment of revelation to know that you are poor and old enough to understand what that means. It propelled me into a life of creating financial security. I started working in my aunt's Dairy Queen at the age of 13 and have never stopped working—babysitting, cleaning apartments, hostessing at a restaurant, waitressing, salad bar attendant in college, etc., etc.

I just didn't want to be the girl who got the "Free Lunch."

When I was young, my mother's grief enveloped our house like a shroud. Many of my earliest recollections involve comforting her and wanting to try to help her be happy. The goal of making my mom happy became a driving force in my life, and I'm sorry to tell you that I have never felt like I succeeded. Prolonged grief and depression have dominated my mother's psyche for as long as I can remember. I have always felt it was my great failure as a daughter not to help my mother achieve happiness. That feeling of inadequacy has subconsciously motivated me to continually try to make others happy. It was so much easier to make other people happy, and it brought me great satisfaction instead of guilt and remorse. I realize now, in retrospect, that it is in the act of pleasing others that I have found what I so desperately craved: affirmation and approval.

The "pattern of pleasing" was set in place at a young age, and I have rarely wavered. I can look back and see the schoolgirl who always got good grades, the teen who worked after school to earn extra money for blue jeans, and the college graduate who took the first job offered to her in copier sales. At the time, I DID NOT want a job selling ANYTHING! I really wanted to be a television journalist.

But... XEROX was a Fortune 500 company, and I had large school loans to pay off.

I decided very impulsively to take the job selling copiers as it appeared to be the right thing to do. I hated the work. The rejection of the sales process was personal to me. I didn't last long in the job, but the position did lead me to the next phase of my journey, as I met my future husband in the sales bullpen.

He was a young successful salesman at XEROX who checked all the boxes. He had a secure job and was the number one salesman at our branch. He was my age and owned a house! Impressive. He was "all-American" handsome. More importantly, all the people I wanted to please in my life approved of him, so marriage seemed like the "right" thing to do.

At the time, I was unsettled, impulsive, full of creative energy, and insecure about the future. He was serious, goal-oriented, and steadfast in his approach to life. It was a good balance. So at the tender age of 23, we got on the "see-saw" of marriage.

I loved him. Was I "in love" with him? I don't think so, in retrospect, as our romance was a true whirlwind. We met in September, were engaged in February, and then married the following September. He had made the ultimate sales pitch—and I had bought it, hook, line, and sinker.

We built a wonderful life together with all the "right" things: a house in a great neighborhood, two cars, two kids, a cat, and a membership at the local country club. I had thrown myself into my married life with fervor. I was the perpetual overachiever and wanted it to be the best it could be.

Not growing up in a traditional household with two married parents, I'd never had the opportunity to observe a married couple. So, I fell into a pattern of doing what my husband asked and expected of me. We followed a very traditional path with "old-fashioned" roles just like his parents. I thought they must have been doing the right thing, so I chose to follow along and not "push the envelope," as my husband would say.

As I look back, I realize that I made a lot of conscious "choices" during my marriage. One of the most significant ones was to put my aspirations on hold and become a mother. I had always wanted children, and I have two sons, whom to this day I consider my greatest accomplishments. I fully embraced motherhood and even made the choice to leave my career as a teacher to be a stay-at-home mom like my mother-in-law. My mother had always worked during my childhood. I recalled not liking having to make my own dinners and never seeing my mom at school like the other homeroom mothers. I wanted it to be different for my kids, and I never regretted being present in my sons' lives and participating fully every step of the way.

There were other "choices" I made to keep things running smoothly. Like the choice to accept an allowance of $800 a month to run my house. The choice to ask permission to use a credit card when making purchases for our home. The choice to keep separate bank accounts with "my money" and "his money," and the choice to maintain the traditional roles where I cooked and cleaned and he cut the grass. But, I also chose to create a beautiful home and make it a gathering place where friends, family, and neighbors were always welcome. I was the "hostess with the mostest" who loved to entertain.

My creative energy was powerful. It overflowed outside my home. I joined the local Garden Club, became PTA president, and organized the neighborhood Bunko Ladies. Yet, it still wasn't enough to satisfy the deep yearnings of my creative soul.

During this time, I started my first business. After retiring from teaching, I missed the creativity of the classroom, so I volunteered to help in my son's kindergarten class. The teacher was brand new and intimidated by my teaching experience. I asked her to let me just come in and tell a story. She agreed. It was October when I entered the classroom dressed as a scarecrow and wowed my audience of little people. My son was so happy. I had to continue. Each month I came up with a new "character" to tell stories. It was the beginning of my 27-year storytelling business, Characters By Kim. It's been a wonderful career that has brought me much joy and touched the lives of thousands of children throughout the years.

Life progressed, and the years passed. I fell (as many do) into a pattern of complacency when things felt good and secure. It's hard to verbalize, but there was still something deep down inside me that was unfulfilled. The urge to do more with my life would sometimes surface, and I would mistakenly "push the envelope."

When both of my boys were in high school, I wanted to go back to college to pursue my Ph.D. in education. I loved teaching and had always wanted to teach new teachers at the college level. I approached my husband about it one day. He said, "Why would we invest any money in you and your education? We have two sons we need to put through college." He was a very goal-oriented planner and had been saving for our sons' educations for many years. I was once again shut down by the voice of reason.

After my oldest son was off to college and my younger son was ready to graduate high school I found myself anticipating them leaving home with dread. It's an unsettling time for a mother. I could see the empty nest scenario coming, and I was not happy that my home would have only me and my husband there. What was I going to do? I just couldn't look at the back of his *Wall Street Journal* every day. I needed *a purpose*, and sure enough, a suppressed aspiration presented itself unexpectedly.

I had always loved "high tea." Something about sipping tea from a delicate china cup and nibbling tiny sandwiches made me deeply happy. I thought it would be so perfect to own a "tea house" of my own, where I could house my storytelling business and host children's birthday parties and also provide a haven for women to gather, discuss books, and take classes and great stuff like that. I had been collecting vintage teacups all my married life. It was the souvenir I sought out when traveling and the treasure I looked for when shopping. I had amassed 65 vintage bone china cups that were all for my "dream tea house."

One day, while driving, I spotted a "for sale" sign on a darling little blue cottage on a very busy road. I called the phone number on the sign and found out the asking price was only $20,000. I went to see it, and oh my, as you can imagine, it needed a lot of TLC! I asked my younger brother to look at it. He said it had good bones, and he would help me with the rehab. I called the borough to make sure I could use the property for my "tea house" purpose.

When all my research was done, I went to my husband to tell him my plan. He dismissed the ideas as *frivolous* and said he didn't care what I did as long as it wasn't with "our" money. His cold response did not extinguish my flickering flame; it only fueled it.

I proceeded to the bank and applied for a $20,000 loan. I remember the day distinctly. The twenty-something banker said, "Can your husband co-sign this loan with you?" I said, "No, I really want to get this loan on my own, please." He lowered his eyes to his papers and said, "I'm sorry, Mrs. Adley, but you're not really worth anything without your husband's name attached."

Kaboom! Bam! Pow!

He had pushed the button that shut down all my systems in disbelief and then rebooted me with a rush of power and purpose. It was the painful and yet purposeful beginning of releasing my soul-level magic.

His words pierced me like a knife. They took my breath away and left me speechless.

He looked up at me when I did not respond and quickly started mumbling an apology... something about not having any credit in my own name, blah, blah, blah. Too late, young man, you have released a beast!!

A mix of feelings rushed through me. I was afraid I would lunge across the table at him or start to cry. I'm not sure how much time passed when I decided to take the high road. I stood up, said "thank you," left, and vowed never to bank there again. If anything, I am resilient. I thought, "I'll find another bank... SCREW HIM!" But his words of worthlessness had struck me in the face like the girl in the lunch line in fifth grade. I would not be called "worthless." I would prove my worth... no matter what.

As it turned out, my older brother offered to lend me the money. Growing up as we did, my brothers and I have a unique, protective bond with one another. I was ready to call the seller again and tell him I had the cash for "my little blue tea house." I drove by the house to take one more look and noticed the "for sale" sign was down. I called the owner, who told me he was sorry, but it was sold. Someone offered him $21,000 and paid in cash just yesterday. I could barely make it home with tears in my eyes. I ran upstairs, threw myself on my son's bed, and sobbed deep wails like someone I dearly loved had died. It was the sudden death of a dream... "my little blue tea house." May it rest in peace.

It was Christmas time when all this was going down, so there was a lot to distract me from the grief of losing my little blue tea house. One of the most important life lessons I learned from my mother is that if you let grief take over your life it can rob you of your purpose. So, I put my many teacups in a box and would later give most of them away. This loss of my dream and the revelation that I had allowed myself to become devalued was the true impetus that led me to embrace my soul-level magic. It did not happen overnight, but through a painful process of loss, change, and reinvention.

My life had been set up like a perfect line of dominos standing in a row, with each element standing precariously balanced side by side. It just took me pushing the first one to set off the chain reaction that knocked them all down in record time.

The new year brought a new me. After Christmas break, the boys went back to college, and the first thing I did was move down the hall into my son's room. I wanted to get my husband's attention and make him realize I was unhappy. This separation under the same roof led to him leaving in March. We filed for divorce in May. He put the house up for sale in June. It sold in one week. I dissolved my marital home of 29 years by myself in six weeks. It was the most painful process I have ever experienced, but it was also cathartic, as I released so many material things I thought were important. I bought my own townhouse in June and was living "on my own" for the first time in my life at the age of 53. The divorce was final in November. It was a complete and total life change in less than a year. My head was spinning.

I kept busy and was back working again as a nanny and a tour guide in Pittsburgh. I was being paid $10 an hour for tours while writing tours and training guides. I knew I could do it better! I researched and found The Center for Women's Entrepreneurship at Chatham University. I started a course called "My Business Start Up" in the dead of winter. It was so dismal driving to campus in the dark and cold, but by the end of the course, it was spring, and I was blossoming with a new business plan for a tour company of my own.

That summer in 2015, at age 54, I filed an LLC for my start-up tourism company called Passport to Pittsburgh, a custom tour design company for Pittsburgh and beyond. I am so proud of my company. It truly embodies so much of me: my ideas, my love of learning, my people-pleasing (in a good way now!), and my creative energy. I started creating one-of-a-kind tours and delivering a product of "experiential tourism" that Pittsburgh had never seen before. My soul-level magic was finally at work... and I have never looked back.

Pittsburgh, Pa., entrepreneur Kim Adley has spent a lifetime engaging others. She holds a BA in journalism from Duquesne University and an MA in teaching from the University of Pittsburgh. After retiring from teaching to raise her two sons, Kim created her professional storytelling business, Characters By Kim. (www.charactersbykim.net) She also worked as a literacy outreach program facilitator and storyteller for WQED Multimedia's Education Department and served as a travel columnist for *Inspiring Lives Magazine*. Kim also engages audiences through her business, Passport to Pittsburgh, LLC., a custom tour design company for Pittsburgh and beyond. (www.passporttopittsburgh.com) The company's "Tourism Trifecta" guarantees *Knowledge, Experiences, and Fun* on every tour. Kim's favorite quote is "*Carpe diem*!"... "Seize the day!"

God's Plan Doesn't Always Look Like the Life We Imagine

By Samantha Bauer

"Go confidently in the direction of your dreams, live the life you have imagined."

~ Henry David Thoreau

This has been my favorite quote since I was a young 20-something with dreams of climbing the corporate ladder and using my high-heeled shoes to bust through the glass ceiling. I loved the thought of chasing my dreams and living the life that I imagined.

But by the time I was in my mid-thirties, I found myself living a life that had parts I had imagined, and parts that I couldn't have possibly imagined.

The killer is that I had worked so hard to get there.

By age 37, I was living the dream... at least from the outside looking in. I was in senior leadership for a large company. I was managing insurance sales for a multi-hundred-million-dollar operation. I had a corner office, a team of about 80 employees who reported to me, a company card, and a six-figure salary. I traveled for business and annual sales incentive trips that I attended as a host to my top sales producers. My extremely supportive husband was holding down the fort at home as a stay-at-home parent to our young kids. I wanted to pave the path in my mission to show my kids, myself, my parents, or whoever I was trying to prove myself to, that mommy could be a fierce businesswoman. And from my Facebook memories that pop up from time to time, I sure did make it look good.

The reality of it, though, was that I was miserable. I was working close to 60 hours per week, six days a week, which left one day a week for my family. I had anxiety because I was being challenged to lead in a way that was very far from every reason I got into leadership. I wanted to lead like Jesus, who I consider to be the greatest leader of all time. Jesus was the originator of servant leadership, the guy who had all the power in the world and chose to use love as his first rule in leadership, who chose to encourage instead of shame. In my mind, he served those who should have been serving him. Jesus didn't tolerate what was bad or wrong or unjust, but he managed to make his points and, I'd go as far as to say, transform the world with love.

I realize I can't literally go around washing my employees' feet! But as leaders, I believe there is so much to learn from how Jesus led (and still leads) people every day to Christianity.

In my corporate position, I was being challenged to lead more like Bobby Knight. Bobby Knight was the Indiana University basketball coach famous for his extreme coaching, doing things like throwing chairs at refs during games, screaming at his players, and utilizing fear as a way to "gain the respect" of his players. This strategy worked well for Mr. Knight. I've read his autobiography (it was a recommendation from my prior manager), and I don't believe him to be a bad person, but definitely not someone I would be comfortable emulating. Fear has never been a leadership strategy I could respect, let alone execute myself; it didn't take long before I couldn't sleep at night and started to really dislike the person I was seeing in the mirror.

The worst part was what I was missing out on at home. I missed every Mother's Day lunch for my kids' preschool. I missed every concert. I had never met their teachers. I never got to see them get on the bus on the first day of school.

Once I took a day off and was so excited to attend a field trip with my son's kindergarten class, but when I got on the bus with him, I was met with deer-in-the-headlight stares from the other moms. My husband had referred to these women as the "mom brigade" due to their non-welcoming attitude toward him as the only stay-at-home dad in the class, and I thought maybe this was their normal greeting. I finally managed to engage in a conversation with one of the other moms, and she awkwardly looked at me and said, "We just assumed that your kids didn't have a mom."

My heart fell into the deepest part of my stomach. They thought I was dead.

In the moment, I very likely did look like a ghost. I'm not speechless often, but all I could do was fake a smile and excuse myself. My son and I still had an awesome day together, but let me tell you, that's a conversation that I will never forget. I wish I could say it was the last "awkward working mom" comment that I've heard, but I've heard them all. And these conversations are the reason that I still, to this day, do not feel comfortable in the pickup line at school or at school events.

Today, instead of being dead to them, I'm that mom who is generally running late, showing up in heels and business attire to the holiday concert, the mom who volunteers to bring the plates to the holiday party when the other moms bring beautify handmade crafts to give to the kids. I can walk into any board room and negotiate with any high-level executive, I can interview candidates, fire employees, and explain insurance coverages to doctors and lawyers, but I am extremely awkward standing in line at the elementary school to pick up my kids.

Go figure.

After the field trip experience, I knew I had to make a change. I felt stuck. I had worked hard for 16 years to move up the corporate ladder and was being courted to become a vice president. I was earning a very comfortable six-figure salary and was the sole income provider for my family. And honestly, I didn't know what to do. My entire career had been in insurance.

Being a Christian and someone who relies on God for all things, I tried to tell myself that God wouldn't have me on this path if it wasn't where I was supposed to be. That he must be using this for me and my family's good. I prayed and cried most mornings on my 35-minute commute downtown and shared with God my desire for change. I prayed and assured Him that I will work for man as though I am working for Him and that I will do His work right where I am if that is where he wants me, but if He did call me elsewhere (*please call me elsewhere, God,* I thought), that I would go.

Isn't it funny that when we are broken down to the point of tears, when we don't know what to do, when we feel truly desperate and finally go to God with that broken-down truth and wholly hand our situations over to Him, he starts talking back?

Let me tell you, he started talking.

Things started getting worse for me at work. My manager at the time was following his own strategy of leading with fear, which made it easy for me to recognize that this was not where God wanted me to be anymore. One night after one of my manager's more animated "coaching" emails, I went home and just unloaded my frustrations on my husband.

"I can't believe this," I vented to my husband, "My team has exceeded our sales goals for the past year-and-a-half, and he told me I am too nice to be an effective sales leader! He literally said that I need to be more of an A-hole. So what? I'm supposed to compromise my character and treat people like garbage to try and squeeze more sales out of them?"

And that's when my then five-year-old daughter walked into the room. She'd overheard me.

"Mom," she said, "You told me never to change who I am for anyone, so you shouldn't either. Don't listen to him; you should be the boss."

I froze. She was 100% right.

She walked back out of the room.

That was the moment that I realized how closely my kids were watching, and I realized I had to make a change.

But, God wasn't done talking to me. Sometimes, he really likes to make his point. About a month after that lightbulb moment with my daughter, a great uncle of mine passed away not long after his 100th birthday. This uncle is one of the last of my grandparent's generation in my family to enter into his time with the Lord. Now, a little background here, my ancestors founded the church that I grew up in. I fondly remember going to church with the back four or five pews on the left side of the church being filled with my grandparents and their siblings, their kids, and me and my brothers and cousins. I passed candy and played tic-tac-toe on the back of church bulletins with grown-ups—usually my grandfather, who is easily one of my all-time favorite human beings.

I arrived late to the funeral and found myself sitting in the pews that I knew so well, by myself, in the very back of the sanctuary. Those pews where I was so used to seeing the people I loved from generations ahead of me now held my dad and his siblings. It was the first time that it had really hit me that the generation that I had adored so much had moved out of this world and onto a better place.

God chose this perfect moment to speak right into my soul. You see, my great uncle and aunt had owned an insurance agency. Their children and grandchildren told amazing stories about memories with my uncle as they grew up. He sang in the church choir, and there wasn't a Christmas Eve service when I don't remember him up there singing praises to God. He was an active volunteer in his community, and even to his final days, he was helping with Meals on Wheels, delivering meals to "old people" as he said, despite the fact that he had 20 to 30 years on some of them.

Somewhere during this service, I felt God's spirit, and it was as though he spoke directly to me. It went something like this, "Hey Sam, when you die, what is your family going to be up there saying about you?" And I thought: *That I worked hard? That I made a lot of money? No, I think what they'd remember is that I wasn't there. They will think that my work must have been more important to me than they were. The people in our church would never really get to know us because I only had time to go to Sunday service. Our community may never be impacted by my existence.*

It was all I could do to hold myself together.

It was as if my grandparents and their siblings were sitting in that empty pew with me, with God sitting between us, just cheering me on. All of them were saying, "Sam, you were created for more than this." I could feel their presence and the warmth of their encouraging love just accepting me for who I am, but also encouraging me to take the amazing examples of love that they had given me, and step into building the life that God had already planned for me. I decided that day that it was time to not just hear the call, but to step into truly being the person God had created. This was a person who would be remembered for making an impact on my kids and their kids and hopefully their kids and their kids.

And so, I started taking action. I had the conversation with my husband that I needed to make a change. I wasn't sure how this would go as he loved being a stay-at-home parent and he was killing it.

We sat down and prayed together more than once about what God's plans might be for us and how we would make a change. We explored some different options in business ownership as well as corporate positions, and quickly determined that God was calling me to open my own agency. We explored all the options available and determined that purchasing a franchise of the largest independent insurance agency in the country made the most sense for us; we could scale quickly and still maintain our independence.

God opened every door that needed to be opened. He put every person in our path who we needed to meet or converse with. He put a job in my husband's hands that would exactly cover our expenses. Even a portion of the capital for our business came from my grandfather's gift that he had left in his estate. I know he is still smiling about this as he watches us grow our business, and more so, watches me grow as a mom, a wife, and a servant of God.

Within three months of my Holy intervention in that back pew of the church I had been baptized and married in, I opened the doors to my insurance agency.

I'll never forget the feeling I had on the evening I gave my notice to my company. As I left that night, I sat in my car and wondered if I was crazy. I sure felt crazy. I had worked for 16 years to climb the corporate ladder, as a female in a male-dominated industry, I had fought so hard to get into the senior leadership position and the income level that I had achieved, yet here I was, 38 years old with a five- and six-year-old at home as the sole income provider for our family, walking away to start over. To add to the kind of crazy that I felt, all I could do was laugh. I sat in my car and laughed and thanked God for what he was going to do for us, for the blessings that I believed He had in store for us, for the courage I felt inside as I took action on His call, for the crazy I felt. I laughed the entire 35-minute drive home. That must be why they call it a leap. Leaps can feel scary and liberating all at the same time.

The thing is that God's plan doesn't always look like our dream. We can try to ignore His call, we can tell Him *no*, and that He's got the wrong person. But (spoiler alert) God always wins. One way or another, His plan for our lives is going to be fulfilled, and we can either do it kicking and screaming, or we can embrace it and take the leap knowing that our big, huge, perfect sovereign God does not make mistakes and He created you specifically to fulfill His amazing plan for your life.

You might be thinking, "Well, Sam, how do we know if the dream in my heart is God's plan for me?" To that I would answer: You know that dream that is tucked way deep down in your heart, the one that sometimes pops into your head that you immediately hush, because you think there's no way that you could achieve it? You make excuses like "it's just a bad time," or "that ship has already sailed," or you just "don't have the right personality," or "you just aren't... [insert self-doubt adjective here] enough"?

You know the dream that you are embarrassed to talk about because it sounds crazy, the one that gives you that flutter in your tummy when you think about it? That's the one. That's what you need to be paying attention to because the fact that you still think about it and that it scares you to pieces and you know that the only way you can achieve it would be by divine intervention is exactly why God wants you to go for it. You can't glorify God if you are staying in your comfort zone, doing things that you could do on your own. The way you are going to glorify God is to do the things that can only be explained by God's intervention.

God wants us to glorify him. He didn't make you and say, "You are almost good." He also didn't put a dream in your heart and then not give you what it takes to accomplish it. You are equipped. Start taking the steps.

I thought I was supposed to climb the corporate ladder and show my daughter that she too someday could break the glass ceiling and live the life she imagines, but God had a better plan for me. He had a better plan for my kids. His plan for me was to build my own ladder, to be an example of love and presence in my family, my church, and my community while building a business that gives so much more to people than the service we provide. His plan included me setting an example just like the one that my grandparents and my parents have set for me.

I won't be there to hear what my family shares about me at my funeral, but I will tell you that they'd have a lot more to say today than they would have three-and-a-half years ago. God willing, by the time He brings me home, my kids and their kids will have so many stories and memories of me that my impact will continue to glorify God for generations after my time on earth has ended. My prayer is the same for you.

Samantha Bauer had been building and leading high-performing teams in the corporate insurance industry since 2005 before opening her own agency, the Bauer Agency of Goosehead Insurance, in April of 2019. Sam has grown her agency to $2 million in written premium in the past three-and-a-half years while being present for her husband and kids, serving her community, and volunteering at her church. She is currently building a team of high-performing individuals with a goal of becoming one of the largest Goosehead franchises in the country.

With a passion for helping others discover a purposeful life, Sam began a podcast in 2021, the Wherever You Go Podcast, where she encourages her listeners to follow the dreams in their hearts to lean into becoming the person God created them to be.

Whether selling insurance, leading a team of high-performing individuals, caring for her family, or serving in her community, Sam's core goal is to represent God in a way that reflects the love and grace of Jesus through her actions onto the people with whom her path gets to cross.

The Three Big Epiphanies that Helped Me Transform My Life

By Elizabeth Craig

About eight years ago I took an unintentional and very deep dive into a five-year period of self-loathing. I had no idea how I got there. I had never been in a place like this before, so when I found myself at the bottom of this dark pit, I was utterly confused.

I also quickly realized that I had zero skills to help navigate my way out of it.

Little by little, I began to understand that my most important relationship was also the most toxic: my relationship with myself. How had I become the kind of woman that couldn't even look at herself as she walked past a mirror? The kind of woman that hurled more nasty insults at herself in her head than any other person ever could out loud? The cultural instructions I had inherited at birth that defined how to live a fulfilled and contented life were present and working like a well-oiled machine.

Perplexed, I mentally scanned through the checklist:

- Graduated college
- Got married
- Bought the house

- Had the child
- Gained financial security

As far as I could tell, I had everything I was told would make a woman happy. So, why was I restless, sad, discontented, and so uncomfortable in every way that it felt like I was crawling out of my skin? I wasn't just baffled; I was annoyed. Who has time for such things? I had a successful business and home to run, a daughter to raise, and a husband with whom to partner in all of it.

Curling up in the fetal position to rock my way out of this was out of the question.

Always having been a driven and tenacious person, I set to work immediately on a seek-and-destroy mission to annihilate the troublesome enemy of self-contempt. A little bit of research identified all the things one must do to love oneself, and I ferociously dove in. Shockingly, starving myself, exercising to death, wearing all the makeup, buying all the clothes, taking all the classes, reading all the books, listening to all the podcasts, and basically panicking myself into Stepford Wifedom didn't work.

I began to understand that I was in the midst of something much bigger than simply needing to make some changes in my life—it was my *entire life* that needed to change. I couldn't help but feel like I was missing some piece of the puzzle that, when discovered and put into place, would bring so much clarity, ease, and relief that I would finally be able to rest, find joy, and have a sense of peace.

Boy-oh-boy was I wrong.

Through an acquaintance, I was told about a woman who worked in Reiki therapy, which I had never heard of. This person raved about the Reiki therapist, named Sharna, and her ability to pinpoint emotional and mental blockages, identify their source(s), and even heal them.

I was so in.

I decided I was done with the feeling that there was something profoundly wrong in my life yet not being able to identify the exact matter of contention; I had reached my limit. So, I did a little research on Reiki, and though I thought it sounded "woo-woo," I was at a place in my life where I would have tried anything for even a moment of respite. As Sharna was, and still is, located in Santa Fe, N.Mex., and I in Pittsburgh, Pa., I set up a distance Reiki session, which was a completely foreign concept to me, and impatiently awaited my healing experience with excitement.

Sharna called on the phone and introduced herself. She ran through a few simple instructions and began her process, which included periods of silence while she worked what I could only have identified as magic. After each quiet stretch, she would come back to the conversation and talk to me about what she discovered, such as issues I had with my father, my childhood, and long-held belief systems that were getting in my way. Slowly, I began to see the puzzle show its picture, and the fog of confusion was lifting. It was like a giant boulder rising off of my chest.

As I realized the events that had shaped and led me to the place I was at that very moment, everything began to make sense.

Then there it was, that last puzzle piece. The answer I had been waiting for. The source of my unhappiness that, now identified, would set me free of my misery. I watched it float down and take its rightful place. And then the boulder crashed back into me so hard the wind flew out of my lungs.

It was my marriage to my husband.

I was in such a state of shock and disbelief that my heart was pounding out of my chest, and I didn't even know where to begin. How in the world did I not know that my marriage was in this much trouble? Where did the initial crack begin that expanded so quietly over the years that it resulted in the eventual shattering of our marriage?

I journeyed back through our relationship to find the source and landed in my seventh month of my first and only pregnancy.

At this time, my husband began telling me about some discomfort he felt in both of his legs right below his knees. In a short period of time, it went from discomfort to numbness and tingling. A visit to our primary care physician indicated that he may have Transverse Myelitis, otherwise known as Neuromyelitis Optica (NMO). A slew of specialists' appointments, coupled with a barrage of MRIs and other tests, confirmed a fate we couldn't wrap our brains around. The prognosis was that he may not survive past the next five years.

He became sick, and I mean *really* sick. He spent months in bed at a time, and the stress that affected him, me, and our home in general, was more than either of us could bear. We had a brand new business that we started when I was two months pregnant, and we were about to move into a brand new house with a brand new baby. Mired in with all of this was the constant reminder that he could die at any moment. This led us to become people that neither of us recognized. I know that two different people in the same relationship can have two very different narratives, but to me, he became resentful and angry, and suddenly, I couldn't do anything right. I saw the looks, heard the judgmental comments, and felt the weight of silent responses that were dripping with disapproval.

I began to understand that I had a perfectly normal and healthy body that I could only assume he believed I didn't deserve, which led to me becoming a target for his fault-finding. The more I was criticized, the more I ate. The more I ate, the more weight I gained. The more weight I gained, the more I hated myself. I began to believe the criticisms were true, and that was my downfall. In turn, I became distant, cold, and angry with him. I pushed him out of my life in every way I could because I always felt as if he was so disappointed in me with regard to, well... everything.

It was a level of pain that left both of us, and our marriage, crippled.

Much later and much too late, I realized that fear was the driving force behind his words and actions. I knew in my heart he held no desire to hurt me. But he was terrified of dying and leaving his wife and young daughter behind, and that despair turned into a need for control. I may not have liked it, but at least I understood it. Unfortunately, he didn't believe we needed help, and looking back, I wish I would've insisted. But, instead of receiving the emotional and therapeutic guidance that we desperately needed, we divided and conquered. We thought we were doing the right thing by "unselfishly" putting everything before our marriage because we never even considered it wasn't strong enough to hold all the pressure and consequences of the disease.

We were wrong.

As my Reiki session came to a close, a sense of dread set in. I knew immediately that it wasn't just that I was having problems in my marriage; it was that my marriage was over. It was as if a cord had been cut the moment the awareness set in, and I had to click the pieces of a new puzzle together to form a permanent path that would become the rest of my life.

I had to weigh the value of continuing the status quo of a life that would keep everyone else around me happy against the expense of my own well-being.

In the end, I decided that the price was too high. Instead, I bet on myself. I bet that if I left, I could begin the return to an even better version of the woman I used to be. I bet that if I left, I could transform my pain into a healthy and loving relationship with myself and be an example to my daughter, showing her that when we need to choose ourselves, we most certainly should. I bet that if I left, I could show her that when we choose ourselves, we are, in essence, being the most selfless we can be to everyone else involved because we can show up as our best selves for our loved ones. I bet that if I left, I could prove to myself that I'm a woman worth fighting for.

Turns out I was a safe bet.

Once I made the decision to leave, I knew I had a long road ahead of me. I understood that my feelings of self-loathing were inextricably tied to my marriage, which meant that I would need to journey with both, simultaneously, to truly heal. I'm happy to say that the journey was well worth the pain. My daughter has two parents that are happy and present, and watching her thrive as a result has been all the proof I need. I'm also deeply grateful that my now-ex-husband and I have a kind and caring friendship.

My wish is that you never find yourself in a place of similar discontent; however, just in case you do, I've chosen one lesson I learned while walking this path to share with you. My hope is that it can be a small part of your guidepost, leading you back to your most authentic and beautiful self.

As I was putting the pieces of myself back together, I kept returning to specific traits of my personality that always made me cringe. I knew that's where I needed to start my work because I also knew I could no longer push parts of myself into the shadows just to make everyone else more comfortable. If I wanted to truly heal, I had to love the whole me, not just the parts others, and myself, found acceptable. Carl Jung calls these traits our "shadows;" I call them my "cringy bits." What I learned about cringy bits is that we are conditioned, typically when we are young, to hide parts of ourselves that are bothersome to others.

When I look back into my childhood, I see a girl who was curious, free, loud, and excited. It didn't take me long to realize that I had been the complete opposite of what the world said little girls were supposed to be. Over time, freedom was replaced with responsibility, loud was replaced with minding my (female) manners, and excitement was replaced with holding it all in and constantly scanning the room to make sure I wasn't offending anyone (I was pretty unsuccessful at this last bit).

I was learning to hate parts of myself that I didn't even know existed yet. I would shove these parts of my personality down, until they reared their ugly little heads right when I least expected it. Then I would internally berate myself for behaving in a way that I was told was unacceptable.

Not surprisingly, as I continued to grow and mature, my cringy bits followed me. Later in life, as I looked back over the journey of my shadow selves, I could see how they grew and matured right along with me. As it turns out, my cringy bits no longer make me cringe, and I figured out something so enlightening to me that it changed my entire relationship with myself—my Three Big Epiphanies. I hope you use them to transform your shadows into something so metamorphic that it causes a rebirth and expansion that has you seeing yourself in a whole different way.

1. **The goal isn't to change, it's to accept.** Humans don't really change, not our core selves. We grow, we evolve, we gain wisdom and knowledge. All of this leads to changes in how we live our lives, but we never truly change our inner selves. We're not supposed to, and if you keep reading you'll understand why, but for now, realize that you don't ever need to change yourself. Rather than putting wasted energy into changing what cannot be changed, use that energy to accept yourself fully and completely, even your cringy bits. My guess is that you've been trying for years to change those parts of yourself, and it's not working. Clearly, a new strategy needs to be developed and maybe this is the time to consider something radical, like loving your whole self.
2. **Your most hated cringy bits are your greatest gifts.** Your cringy bits may feel cringy right now, but that's only because you haven't learned how to transform them into your greatest superpowers yet. You've been gifted this legacy; you just haven't figured out the delivery yet in a way that's going to serve you and others, big time. Therefore...

3. **Rather than sending your cringy bits anger and hatred, send them love and gratitude.** Because when you are sending darkness and disgust, you are not only evolving them with darkness and disgust but you are also keeping them separate from your complete self, and so long as you live fractured in this way, you will never be whole. We've now learned that our cringy bits can't be changed and that they are actually our greatest gifts. Would you ever tell someone that their greatest gifts deserved anything less than infinite love and gratitude? This is how we become whole, and only with love and gratitude can we transform our weaknesses into strengths.

What others believed were traits that needed to be banished were actually traits that have led me to my greatest purpose. Little did I know that, through my photography, I would spend the better part of the last two decades of my life becoming a guide to women in the midst of reckoning with their inner selves. Most recently, adding Reiki and intuitive coaching to my skillset has allowed me to journey deeper with women. It has been my greatest joy to help them unravel and peel away their own social conditioning to reveal a version of themselves they never knew was lying in wait underneath everyone else's expectations. Leading women to rediscover the courage they've always had inside of them and helping them design their lives to be in alignment with their truest and most authentic selves has been the most fulfilling thing I've done in my life.

Looking back, I now recognize that I was wrongly informed in regards to the so-called unacceptable traits of my personality—and even worse than being told these things, I *believed* what I was told. This led to an attempt to contort my square self into a round hole while trying to conform to cultural norms I had no participation in constructing. Even with all of that, I found the strength to come full circle, gathering the pieces of my personal puzzle back up that I had so mistakenly and willingly scattered.

I accepted my complete self. I transformed what was labeled as undesirable into my greatest gifts. I now live a life of wholeness, celebrating every part of myself.

Yes, *every* part!

If you're struggling with your personal journey of self-love, I want to share a bit of advice that I hope you call upon when you need it the most.

1. **The pursuit of self-love isn't easy, but it's worth it.** You must remember at all times that you're a beautiful soul having a human experience, and the greatest gift you can give to yourself is *forgiveness.* Never keep from yourself what I'll bet you give freely to others.
2. **Never question that you are exactly where you're supposed to be** at exactly this moment in time, doing exactly what you're supposed to be doing. You are enough. Always.

3. You have everything you need inside of you to live your most joyous and inspired life, and you always have. Never forget it.

Welcome to the journey, friend. Xx

Elizabeth Craig

Intuitive Life Coach | Reiki Practitioner | Photographer

Through all of Elizabeth's favorite creative talents, she has positioned herself to help women dig deep, rediscover their confidence, and align their choices, decisions, major life events, and shifts with their highest and best good. Her free-spirit approach to life and genuine, authentic nature is what allows her to intimately connect with her clients and subjects.

The merging of self-love with healing as a service began with Elizabeth's photography career, helping women uncover and honor their inner beauty by taking them on a visual journey with their outer beauty. As her photography career progressed in the area of self-love, the desire to help women more deeply led her to the paths of Reiki, teaching, and coaching, all with the central focus on healing the soul.

Elizabeth specializes in combining intuitive life coaching with Reiki therapy in an effort to help women heal their emotional blockages while providing guidance and leadership in their personal life journeys. This is all with the goal of loving the self, evolving the self, but most importantly, designing and living an authentic life to honor the self.

Circle Back to Now

By Sue E. Fattibene

It took me years to find the internal rhythm that allowed me to trust my intuition and step into my calling as a life coach. My life as I know it today has been filled with crazy syncopations, intricate rhythms, soulful ebbs and flows, and dynamic crescendos. I like to compare this to the incredibly beautiful *Piano Concerto No.2 Op.18* by Rachmaninoff.

I learned to play piano by ear when I was a child. I started by listening to my sister play songs she learned in piano lessons. After she finished practicing, I would sit down and play the songs I had just heard her playing without reading the music.

When my parents gave me piano lessons, I did not enjoy playing the piano as much as I had previously—there was too much structure. I *can* read music but struggled to read it. Until college, the music itself was a lifeline for me, a tempo builder, a confidence booster. But to this day, reading music and remembering music theory is a struggle.

Music has always been in my blood, though.

As a senior in high school, I was a drum major, a flute player, and a drama student with leads in musicals. I attended Alabama Girls State and was president of the National Honor Society. I was accepted into Alabama's All-State Choir and All-State Band. Mr. Walters, my band director, selected me to receive the annual John Philip Sousa Band Award at our band's end-of-year celebration. I really knew music, and I was a successful overachiever in life at the young age of eighteen!

I graduated from high school with a full scholarship to Baptist College at Charleston in South Carolina, to study music therapy. I thought this would be the break I needed to learn new musical techniques and apply them as an up-and-coming music therapist. I was excited about what was ahead. I felt like I was on fire with my whole world lit up before me. I could see clearly. The music of inspiration, knowledge, and opportunity was like a beautiful orchestra playing in my head, giving me cues on how to move forward as a young adult. I could find my tempo and walk to the beat of my internal drum, my heartbeat, my intuition.

When I began the music therapy program, I learned I would be a trailblazer in this field, as it was a newly emerging field of employment. But even though I knew music and was a "successful overachiever," I was far from home and did not have my family or trusted high school advisors nearby cheering me or supporting my decisions. At first, I couldn't wrap my head around just how "trailblazing" I would have to be.

Across the street from my college was a convalescent center that partnered with the school and offered internships. In my sophomore year, I was given the opportunity to be an intern at the center. It was eye-opening to see how music can be used as therapy to help someone mitigate their life issues.

One of the patients I worked with at the center was my friend's sister. She was a quadriplegic due to a car accident, and her prognosis was not good. I worked with her and others, using music as therapy. We'd play music, sing, and shake instruments. It is amazing to see people come alive emotionally, verbally, or physically when they hear a song. But my friend's sister did not respond to the music.

It hurt my soul to see her this way.

When she passed away, my heart hurt, and my vision for music therapy began to slip. I could not make sense of the situation. I had someone's delicate life in my hands, and because I would have to work hard to prove myself in this relatively new industry, I was not sure I could cut it. How could I assert myself as I was told I would need to do, especially when I felt like I had already failed? It felt daunting and overwhelming.

With all the uncertainties around this industry and my experience during this internship, I decided I would not pursue music therapy any longer. My heart grieved what I thought would be my career. Now, there was a vacant void, a loss of career opportunity at the age of 20.

By nature, I was not a risk taker, and after what I experienced, music therapy was too big of a risk. I gave up my scholarship and walked away from my future career, completing step one toward my non-risk-taking life. Playing it safe.

"What would be next?" I wondered. When I walked away, I felt some of my life music fading in my soul. It was like this moment at 19 minutes and 34 seconds into the YouTube video of *Piano Concerto No.2 Op.18 featuring Anna Fedorova*, where the piano keys twitter beautifully and then the orchestra goes silent. In the quiet interim where I pondered my next steps, my internal tempo seemed to slip and my syncopation got a little off.

After I decided to forfeit this opportunity, I picked up an MRS degree—that's "Mrs." if you didn't know. I left school in May and by September of that year, I married my first husband. This was step two toward my non-risk-taking life.

Fast forward seventeen years. I was married and a banker. I finally finished my college education in my mid-thirties and received a bachelor of science degree in human resource management with an intensive minor in business from Southern Wesleyan University in Central, S.C. During this time, I had endless nights of studying and learned that listening to classical music helped me study, concentrate, and comprehend information. I happened upon a Rachmaninoff CD at the store, and it became one of my favorites to listen to as I studied.

In particular, from that CD, I found *Piano Concerto No.2 Op.18* to be therapeutic. I could not get enough of this concerto! It is like it was written for my soul sharing my life story from beginning to end. I found myself moving into a curious musical awakening when I pursued my bachelor's degree for the second time. Standard classical music, classical guitar music, and jazz music really met me at the root of who I am and began to light a new fire in me. I saw how my soul stirred, and my learning was successful as I completed my degree because of the music.

While finishing my degree, I took an online class with Dr. William Glasser, a professor at Texas Tech University. He was the creator of Choice Theory, a school of thought that teaches that individuals have an innate ability to control what they do, and therefore can make viable choices that affect the necessities of life. I came alive with his teachings and wanted to work with others to help them make choices to positively move forward in what they wanted to do for their lives personally and professionally. I awakened to how this could benefit and impact so many!

Realizing that you have control over your choices in life is a magical concept. It may not work for all, but it should work for most if they are willing to give it a try.

But once I had my degree in human resource management and an understanding of Choice Theory, what would I do with it?

I continued to be a banker while this powerful information just sat there within me, itching to get out.

Four years after I achieved my degree, I was divorced. I felt my syncopated tempo and the music of my soul diminish once again. I was trying to make sense of emotional discord with a life from which I walked away and was learning new talents as a single parent, while trying to manage everyday life as best I could personally, spiritually, professionally, relationally, financially, and so much more. I knew that I made a great living for my daughter and me as a banker; the job paid our mortgage, put food on the table, helped me save for an occasional vacation, and kept us steady on the course of step three toward my non-risk-taking life.

One day, though, I had a revelation. I found balance when I turned on music, laughed, danced, and cleaned the house with my daughter. I knew, like the beautiful concerto at 23 minutes and 44 seconds with a silent interlude just before the crescendo, my life had meaning and purpose, and the music of my soul was beginning to come alive again.

The silent interlude felt like I inhaled *all the things* and exhaled the goodness of life again.

Five years later, God provided me with the amazing man who became my husband. I was a new bride blending a family and turning chaos to happiness! Unfortunately, one and a half years after we married, I found out I had cancer. This journey was tough and painful, with treatment and six surgeries, full of crazy soulful dreams and visions, embellished with recovery, and it really woke me up! I realized from those dreams during this time that I would not be a banker anymore and was then on a path to discover what my true calling would be.

I meditated, prayed, asked God so many questions, and learned that my soulful gut had so many answers for me. During these cancer-laden years, I actually trusted myself to listen intuitively and follow what I was sensing. At the end of my cancer journey, all in one week, I left my banking career of over 26 years, was released from my surgeon, and jumped on a plane to a destination where I would be trained as a life coach. It was like the rush of the crescendo in the concerto at 28 minutes and 3 seconds! Talk about a wave of rapid life change in multiple ways with massive risk-taking at the Conductor's helm and embrace!

I knew life coaching was my new purpose in life, and it was worth the risk of leaving my safe banking career to become my own boss as an entrepreneur. It was time to change lives as I was stepping out of that guarded life to transform into this new, brilliantly syncopated soulfully intuitive song of life and love to share with the world.

In reflection, learning advanced music theory was painful for me. It was almost like the bad apple that ruined the good apples in the lovely basket. I just could not go there in my brain, as that was not how God designed me to hear His music for me to play. As a young adult, I walked away from music. It was like I could not hear it innately anymore, as I had as a child when I would intuitively play the piano without sheet music or formal training. It was as if my music had gone dark—no drumming in the distance, a silent void.

But there is good news. The download of music did not leave me. It took years, life experiences, and spiritual growth in my relationship with God that allowed for the internal flow of music to come back to me stronger than ever before.

As I circle back to now, I have learned that His music in my head is not always for my use in the real world. It is more for me as meditation, inspiration, and my connection with Him. It is my God Therapy Time. I got the beautiful ebbs and flows of melodic syncopation back. Now I love to sit down at the piano to allow free-flow meditation to happen. At the end of those sessions, I am always amazed by what comes out of my mind, through my soul, to my fingertips as they dance along the ivories. The creativity that comes to me is powerful and awe-inspiring. Sometimes when I finish playing the piano, my creativity in other facets of my life comes to life, swelling in beauty and fullness.

I recently decided in personal meditation time spent with God to focus on why I walked away from my calling in college. After all, it was an important moment, leading to quieting the music and not trusting my younger self's intuition.

This is what came to me:

"You did not feel safe to step out and do something unusual. You felt you needed to walk in the old traditional work method of 8 AM to 5 PM, Monday through Friday. Doing the unfamiliar was so uncomfortable that you gave up the scholarship to be trained in music therapy. You did not like the music theory training; maybe because I blessed you with an ear to hear music and the ability to play music by ear. So, you walked away from music for years until one day music called you back to it and it became your 'ear' again. You then became comfortable just playing, singing, or sitting in what came out of you musically through your soul, through your fingers, to your flute, piano, bongos, and your voice. You began hearing melodically and harmonically in its purest form, and you play in that manner or sing in that manner with comfort."

During this meditation time, these definitions were succinctly spoken to me:

"Harmony—the contribution of strength and support for other musicians."

"Life Coaching—the contribution of strength and support for individuals."

Then, I heard these words:

"I called you to this, Sue. Life coaching was where you needed to be the colorful harmonic vessel of support for others. You could not sit idle anymore. It was okay that you were not ready for music therapy. Yet, I needed you there. But through life's experience, I circled you back to your music, leadership, and counsel as a life coach to walk with others as their cheerleader, accountability partner, and their vessel who would guide them. When you moved into your music again and into coaching, I knew, through life's experiences, you had been groomed and were ready this time for what I had for you to do on this part of your journey in life."

Needless to say, when I heard this, I burst into tears!

What would I have changed when I was younger if I could today? I wish I would have had the courage to trust myself and step out in what I felt I was called to instead of letting others tell me what I should and should not do. That I would have trusted my instincts, my God-given intuition, to follow through in what was being presented to me instead of walking away. Who knows where I would have been today if I had stayed on my path instead of selecting the non-risk-taking life?

However, what I learned over time is that a calling changes in life. And God had a way to circle me back to music and incorporate it into my life personally, spiritually, and professionally. He is the grand Conductor of life, and I am grateful He moves me in this melodic, harmonious, orchestral way to be there for those whose life's scenarios turned the music down and threw them off tempo. That I have the privilege to help them find their balance and authentic syncopations to crescendo in life with their dreams, goals, and visions.

Today, in life coaching and speaking and at the conferences and retreats I create, I use the content I created while listening to music to inspire and motivate others to find their flow and balance in life. I have learned that music moves all of us at different tempos, syncopations, and levels of musical artistry. It allows us to receive emotions and strength to move beyond what we realize we are capable of.

I learned to trust myself and to be willing to allow the spiritual flow of God to resound within my soul. Understanding this thought was like the turn of the concerto, at 34 minutes and 30 seconds, in the moment of my life which led to the copasetic melodic flowing movement. I stepped out of my non-risk-taking life, and into all the risks of trusting my soul with spiritual intuition and being guided through chaos and uncertainty by trusting God to teach me how to ebb and flow the right way so I would become the vessel I was scripted to be for His service for others on this earth.

Finally, that incredible ending to the concerto, at 35 minutes and 46 seconds, is SO flowing, intense, powerful, melodic, moving, and inspirational! The musicians played with such intensity, and they had intrinsic trust for the Conductor who moved the orchestra through this gift of music with the intention of inspiring the audience. It takes my breath away every single time I listen to it.

Young adult Sue can rest assured that as she circles back to now, she will find me, mature adult Sue, finally doing exactly that which my great Conductor has called me to do with a beautiful upbeat balance of blending music, therapy, leading, and life coaching together. It has generated strong internal rhythms and beats within my intrinsic and intuitive soul so I may rise and be the vessel I am called to be for many on this great earth.

Sue Fattibene is the CEO of Rev Up! with Sue. She is a certified international life coach, business strategist, inspirational speaker, conference creator, bestselling author, and artist. She has 26+ years of experience in banking, financial underwriting, and business strategies, and 11 years of experience in life coaching. She holds a bachelor's degree in human resource management with an intensive minor in business.

In her memoir, *The Day the Angel Sat Beside Me ~ A Story of God's Promises Fulfilled in the Midst of the Storm,* she shares her journey from cancer to calling. She also co-authored a book, *Divine Direction*, with inspirational stories of transformation in the lives of twenty-two authors.

Connect with Sue Fattibene in the following ways:

Email revupwithsue@gmail.com

Website www.suefattibene.com

Personal Facebook page @suefattibene

Facebook business page @suefattibeneexceptionallife

Instagram @songbird_sue

LinkedIn Sue Fattibene

Paris is Always a Good Idea

By Kelly Frost

Audrey Hepburn once said, “Paris is always a good idea.”

When I first heard this quote some time ago, I thought: That sounds like a nice sentiment, but it will never be me. That will be one of those bucket list items that never gets checked off. I’ll probably just live vicariously through other people’s social media posts and be completely jealous for the rest of my life!

When I was 39, I was working with a client who was going to attend a conference in Paris and asked if I wanted to be her plus one. We were in the middle of her launch and didn’t want to lose momentum, so we intended to work when she was not tied up in the conference.

I’ve heard people talk about how their hearts skipped a beat when they met someone or something wonderful happened to them. I never really understood that, until that moment. When she asked me if I wanted to spend a week in Paris with her, I could feel my heart skip a beat. I instantly pictured myself in front of the Eiffel Tower, wearing a beret and a French outfit with an umbrella (clearly this was my French image at the time).

But this vision of bliss didn't last long. It was May and I had two school-aged children. My mind started to race...

Can my current husband and ex-husband work together to make sure the kids' day-to-day lives will be taken care of? Is this financially feasible? I am deathly afraid of flying, and this is roughly an eight-hour international flight... can I do that? I don't have a passport. Hell, I don't even speak French!

I told my client I would discuss it with my husband and let her know by Monday. Truly, I needed to explore the negativity in my head first and see if I could overcome it before I even thought about having that talk with my husband. It took me a little bit of time, but I decided I could figure everything out, all the barriers that seem insurmountable and as large as the Eiffel Tower itself. Could I get past them?

It was FEAR that had me frozen. The FEAR of flying, the FEAR of traveling basically alone (she was in first class, I was in coach). She would be gone six hours a day at a conference, and I would be alone most days. I have never taken public transportation before, not a Pat bus, not the T, not even one of those group pedal beer vehicles, and now I would need to take the Paris metro!

There was tons of FEAR behind these thoughts.

I grew up a tad inexperienced. My parents were not fans of anything outside of the South Hills of Pittsburgh. My image of Downtown Pittsburgh growing up was that of a scene straight out of the Batman movie when the Joker chases you down an alley at gunpoint, robs you, and shoots you. My mother had a way of transferring her fears (both valid and neurotic) to me. That transference never stopped, even as I grew into adulthood.

Eventually, I cleared my head and decided I wasn't going to let the fear stop me. Who was I kidding? This was an opportunity to go to Paris! My husband already made it clear that he had absolutely no interest in ever visiting France, so I knew he wouldn't care that I wasn't going without him. So, that was it; I was going!

I made a list of everything I needed to do, learn, and prepare before I left, and I was off!

The flight was comical! Before it, I'd had a margarita at TGI Friday's, along with Dramamine, Imodium, and a Xanax, in an attempt to get comfortable enough to even get on the plane. Did I mention that I get motion sickness? While my client eased into first class, the couple that was supposed to be seated in my row took one look at me and requested to move to a different part of the plane. (They probably thought a crying baby would be a better companion than me. I can't disagree.)

Halfway through the flight, we hit some horrific turbulence that lasted for quite a long time. Once the seatbelt sign was turned off, my client immediately came back to check on me, knowing how I feel about flying. She was ready to calm me down and stay with me for a while, which was so sweet. However, I slept through the entire thing! We are talking *Weekend at Bernie's* behavior from me at this point. If she hadn't told me about the turbulence, I would have never known!

I arrived in Paris totally rested and ready to go, and we hit the ground running!

I am beyond a Type A personality, so I had taken French lessons online before we left to learn as much of the language to get by as I possibly could. "Where is the bathroom," and "I'd like a glass of wine," were at the top of my list, and I had them down! We went through customs and checked into the hotel as soon as we arrived. The hotel was so chic! However, the rooms were tiny, and of course, the TV was in French.

My client's afternoon was going to be consumed with a meet and greet for her conference. I decided to unpack and put everything away—this is a bit of a travel ritual for me, as order seems to bring me comfort.

She returned, and I was chomping at the bit to get out of the room and explore! We were within walking distance of The Arc de Triomphe which is at the end of The Champs-Elysees. We took a stroll, stopped at a famous café, and had an early dinner with wine. (Every meal, including breakfast, included wine, which is basically more affordable than a can of Coca-Cola in France.)

Next, we strolled the streets just in awe of everything and ended at the Arc where we (and every other tourist there) were taking an ungodly number of photos.

After walking back to our hotel, my client spent some time on the phone in the lobby with her loved ones, and it gave me a chance to call home too. Everyone in Pittsburgh was doing great, and I was told not to worry and to enjoy this time. It really was the first time I had ever traveled without a parent, a husband, or a child. No one was depending on me, and I didn't have to check in with anyone.

It felt like pure freedom, and I had four more days of it!

The next day, my client went about her day at her conference. I was ready to explore... and eat, but I had to decide how I was going to travel within Paris. Walk? Motorcycle? Taxi? Metro? I started with the taxi, but there is a lot of traffic, and it gets expensive quickly! I decided to get a metro card—yes, me, the girl that had never taken public transportation before, was about to go underground in a foreign city and take the metro!

Have you ever heard someone talk about having a couple of alcoholic beverages for some "liquid courage"? Just traveling to Paris gave me liquid courage! After my first ride, I took a selfie so I could always remember the feeling I had. I'll admit I was a little nervous, I didn't know exactly where I was going, they were speaking in a language that was not native to me, and I was alone. But dammit, I was in Paris and FEAR was not stopping me from anything!

I went to lunch by myself and loved it! I was able to communicate in French... it was completely broken and

Americanized, but I was able to communicate. I found restrooms, wine, and could order food... I had the basics down!

My destination that day was the Pere Lachaise Cemetery. I was so excited to have a quiet, peaceful day there. I planned to walk the grounds and just reflect. That is exactly what I did. I knew that Jim Morrison was laid to rest there and that was something I wanted to see, but after researching, I was amazed by all the other incredibly talented people who had passed away and were laid to rest there. It may sound strange to some, but I felt it was an honor to pay my respects to them. Each gravesite told a story reflective of that person's life and it was so interesting, and truly moving. It made me feel even more grateful to be on that trip.

I was standing in front of the final resting place of Oscar Wilde, Moliere, Chopin, Edith Piaf, Sarah Bernhardt, Marcel Marceau, Honoré de Balzac, Richard Wright, Amadeo Modigliani, Ettore Bugatti... and this is just to name a few! Not to mention the absolute beauty of the actual cemetery. It is a work of art itself. I truly was in awe the entire time. It was a very moving experience.

That day reinforced my understanding that life is precious and short, and that every day is a blessing. The message was clear: I really needed to start living my life to the fullest and stop hiding my light because it may be too bright for some.

The next two days, my client and I were able to spend some time touring Paris together. We visited the Eiffel Tower and the Tower Gardens... we even ate at the restaurant at the top of the tower! The Louvre was incredible, seeing the *Mona Lisa* that close is a completely different experience. We toured Notre Dame Cathedral when a mass was taking place. We did some shopping on The Champs-Elysees, I commemorated my trip with a little blue box from Tiffany's, we took a sunset cruise on the Seine River, put our locks on the bridge and threw the keys in the water, and we ate, and ate, and ate.

I've never had so much wine and crème brûlée in my life! I have no regrets!

I spent the last day there by myself. My entire life I've loved horticulture. When doing my research on Paris attractions, I came across the Luxembourg Gardens. My client had no interest in this (or the cemetery—in fact, she thought I was a bit strange for wanting to see that), so I saved Luxembourg for the last day in Paris when I'd be alone.

It couldn't have been a more perfect day. I awoke that morning feeling excited for what the day would bring, excited for our last dinner together when her conference concluded, and excited to head home because I was missing my hubby and kids.

The weather was incredible, and that was crucial because I was going to be outside all day in the Luxembourg Gardens... the grounds are huge! There are over 100 sculptures in the gardens, including a miniature *Statue of Liberty*. The plants and flowers were gorgeous, and the aroma was intoxicating. I could have spent days there!

I approached a midway point in the gardens, and there was an enormous gazebo encircled with benches. As I got closer to it, I could see that there were chairs inside the gazebo and what looked to be high school- or college-aged students sitting down. It was in a beautiful part of the garden, and I decided to take a rest and sit down on a bench.

Within minutes I started to hear music.

It was very soft at first and then louder, I could now see that the students inside the gazebo were part of an orchestra, and they were performing. The music was familiar and as it got louder, I could make it out. They were playing *All You Need Is Love* by The Beatles! I know my mouth hung open in disbelief as I looked around this immaculate Garden in Paris where I was sitting on a random bench and an orchestra out of nowhere started to play The Beatles... and WELL, I might add.

I remember thinking to myself "this is my life," and then thinking "this is just the beginning." I started to cry, and when I say I'm not one who cries, I'm not one who cries. I'm typically pretty stoic. It's not that I'm not extremely caring, but that phrase "stop crying, or I'll give you something to cry about" kind of stuck with me at some point, and unless something is really wrong (or really right, in this case) my eyes tend to stay dry.

This entire scene seemed like it was straight out of a movie. As Oprah exclaims often, this was an *aha* moment! I was offered this opportunity, and instead of letting FEAR stop me as I have so many times before. Instead of letting all those voices from the past that told me time and time again that I wasn't good, smart, educated, or thin "enough" rule my decisions, rule my thought process, and rule my self-esteem...

I decided to ignore them.

I decided those voices are flat-out *wrong*.

Most of the time, there is a reason that others speak negatively about someone else, and most of the time, it has nothing to do with the other person! The person who is being critical really thinks that *they* aren't good enough, smart enough, educated enough, or thin enough. The criticizer doesn't know what to do with their feelings, so they project them onto someone else. Unfortunately, often it is children who bear the brunt of this criticism.

I found my strength in Paris. I arrived a little apprehensive but hopeful. Being alone, I had a chance to find myself again. I got the opportunity to discover who I was becoming, what I wanted to stand for, and what kind of path I wanted to walk in life. I left many voices from my past in France, and the next opportunities that came my way when I returned were much easier to say YES to because I had learned how to believe in myself again, how to speak to myself again, and yes, how to love myself again.

Perhaps it is true that *all you need is love*—but there is one thing I know for certain: Paris is *always* a good idea.

The founder & CEO of FROST Executive Services, Kelly Frost has more than 20 years of thriving success in the fields of consulting, strategic planning, management, marketing and advertising, branding, publishing, media production, communications, event planning, and human resources.

In 2022 Kelly launched PEEL: Pittsburgh's Elevated & Emerging Leaders. PEEL was formed around philanthropic endeavors. Every event, luncheon, happy hour, etc., is tied to charitable giving. PEEL's mission is to provide immediate relief and focus on helping people with their obstacles over the long term. Its members do this by collecting/delivering donations and monetary contributions, sponsoring and attending events, and physically volunteering where needed. PEEL members want to make the world a better place one act at a time.

During the pandemic, in the position of assistant executive director, Kelly elevated a woman's networking group after she successfully spent a year as the Pittsburgh director.

She co-facilitated the launch of a national publication, *Inspiring Lives Magazine* (*ILM*), a magazine with an emphasis on business, lifestyle, health & wellness, travel, and much more. The magazine became widely sought after and was nationally available in Barnes & Noble, Books-a-Million, online, and through subscription. *ILM* was the magazine of The Global Sisterhood 501(c)(3) where Kelly sat on the executive board.

While working to have her passion match her purpose, Kelly discovered there was a book on her heart, and from that, she began *A Toast to Motherhood: The Good, The Bad, & The Hilarious*. The book is a collection of stories from Kelly and women in her life who have stories to share about their (real life) experiences with motherhood. Her intent for the book is that she provides entertainment, inspiration, encouragement, laughter, connections, empowerment, and strength and has the ability to support these women and contribute to some phenomenal charities.

In 2017, after temporarily losing partial vision and hearing, Kelly underwent weeks of testing where she was ultimately diagnosed with multiple sclerosis (MS). Rather than allowing this disease to define her, she decided to be an advocate for those who share her diagnosis. Kelly is now on the National Multiple Sclerosis advisory board, lending her voice, her story, and her talents in any capacity to assist those with MS and those with loved ones fighting MS. Kelly was also the keynote speaker for the MS Society's yearly fundraising luncheon in September at the Heinz History Center.

Kelly is a native of the South Hills in Pittsburgh, Pa., and is a graduate of Penn State University in the field of industrial and organizational psychology.

Daddy's Girl, Sam

By Denise Ann Galloni

As a young girl growing up in the '70s, my life was uneventful. I had two loving parents who always had time for me. My mother was a stay-at-home mom who always participated in school activities. I loved being in the kitchen when she cooked and baked. I'm sure I was a great help!

My father sold real estate and then moved on to selling cars. His schedule was anything but routine, but he loved spending time at home with his family. I still remember him teaching me how to hit a golf ball even though the club was taller than me. I always laughed and had a good time with my dad. I was Daddy's girl for sure. His nickname for me was "Sam." I have no idea why he liked to call me Sam; he never explained it. I was Daddy's girl, Sam.

When I was eight years old, my sister was born. There was such joy when my parents finally had their second child to shower with love.

My middle school was nearby, and I had lots of friends to walk back and forth to school with. I liked school; it was a different time when kids were not faced with the same type of issues they face today, like bullying and violence.

Life was good... until it wasn't.

It still amazes me how life can change in the blink of an eye. Time stops, and when it restarts, you try to live the rest of your life in that new normal. As a child, you don't understand the gravity of what has happened or how your future has been changed for the worse.

To this day, my family always teases me about my memory (or lack of one). I have a terrible memory, but that horrible night in 1974 is etched in my brain.

It was a regular weeknight, nothing special at all. My mother, my father, and I finished dinner. My sister was only 18 months old, so she was fed her baby food earlier. My mother cleaned off the table and carried all the dishes to the kitchen. I put my schoolbooks on the table, and it was time for my least favorite activity, homework! A typical boring night.

I sat at the table working on my homework, while my dad was playing with my sister in the living room and my mother was upstairs getting things ready to give my sister a bath and put her to bed. I watched them from my spot at the dining room table. He was lying on the couch and lifting her over his head into the air while she was laughing that cute laugh that babies do. He looked so happy; his family meant everything to him. I could tell there was no place he would rather be than with his children.

I was so happy. Life was good. I loved my new little sister, and felt that, after having been an only child for eight years, my family was now complete.

As I tried to work on my homework, I was laughing at all the crazy sounds and noises my dad was making as he played with my sister, trying to make her giggle. I did not want to do my homework at all. I wanted to play too, as any 10-year-old would. If I'd had a crystal ball to see the next few hours, I would have thrown my books aside and spent time playing with them. I would have really enjoyed the last bit of normalcy with my little family while life was good.

While I was sitting there, I noticed that my dad's playful noises changed. I laughed because I thought they were silly-sounding noises I'd never heard him make before. When I got older, I realized he had been gasping for air, but I was too young to comprehend what was happening at the time.

My mother ran down the steps, screaming his name in a panic, "Bob, *Bob*!" She grabbed my sister, pushed her into my arms, and told me to go upstairs, close the bedroom door, and not come out until she told me to come downstairs.

I was so scared; I had no idea what was going on and how things changed from laughing and happy times to this. I never saw my mother screaming like that. She was frantic. My sister started crying, she must have been able to sense something bad was happening. I still didn't realize what was going on.

We were upstairs behind a closed door in the bedroom for a long time. I don't know how long, but it seemed like forever. We could hear commotion and noises downstairs. It's strange that I can remember all these details to this day but have no idea what we did while we were in that bedroom waiting for my mother or father to call us back down. I don't even remember whose bedroom we were in.

Looking back almost fifty years later, I think I went into shock because I could not process what was occurring. I was so scared. I don't remember if I was crying or what happened until we were called back downstairs.

Eventually, I heard a woman yell up the stairs for me to come down and bring my sister. The voice sounded comforting, and I thought everything would be okay—I could just go back to my homework, and my dad could play with my sister. I remember feeling so relieved as I was walking down the steps, carrying my sister. When we came downstairs, my mother and father were gone, and our next-door neighbor was sitting on the couch. She told me my mother took my father to the hospital because he was sick, and my aunt was coming over to get us until they came home.

I hoped my dad would be OK. He was never sick. I couldn't figure out why my mother couldn't stay with us while he went to the hospital himself, or why we couldn't go too.

A few minutes later, my aunt, uncle, and two cousins came to pick us up to go for a ride. It seemed like we drove around all night. It was late and dark outside. I was getting sleepy and just wanted to go home, see my parents, and go to bed. I kept thinking about how tired I would be when I had to get up the next morning and get ready for school. Each time we passed my house, the lights were still off. That meant my parents were still not back from the hospital, so we continued to drive around.

Finally, we pulled up to my house, and it looked like every light was on. I jumped out of the car and ran to the front door, while my uncle was trying to hold me back until we could all go in together. No one knew what to expect. Well, I think my aunt and uncle knew it was bad, very bad. As soon as we walked into the house, I saw my mother. That's when I knew something bad was going on.

My mother just sat there with a look on her face I had never seen before, holding one of my dad's favorite slippers. No one said a word. We all sat there in silence. Even my sister was quiet in my uncle's arms. After what seemed like a long time, she called me over to her lap, started to cry, and whispered "Daddy died."

Instantly, my aunt ran over and hugged us.

I couldn't process what was happening. *Only old people died,* I thought; *my dad was only 39*. He had just been laughing and playing with us a few hours ago. Christmas was coming and the only thing I could think of was his gifts and how it would work if Daddy wasn't here. How would we buy presents when my mother didn't have a job?

I don't remember how it happened, but the next memory was being at my grandparent's apartment later that night. My dad's parents were also in shock, but they had to step in and help us. My mother didn't know what to do. That night we stayed with them. I can still remember hearing my pap making phone calls when he thought I was asleep, letting people know that his son was gone.

The next few days were a blur: not going to school for days, being at the funeral home, seeing him lying in the casket looking like he was sleeping, and family coming to see us. After the funeral, everyone piled into our house for the wake.

My life changed the moment I heard the words, "Daddy died."

It changed in part because we always struggled financially after that. I remember my mother telling me there was no money to buy me school clothes or goodies from the store—we only had enough for the necessities. I was so afraid something was going to happen to my mother, and we would be taken away to live somewhere else separately. I was scared I might never again see the sister I loved so much.

My friends didn't understand, they all had mothers and fathers. They would go on vacation, but we could never go anywhere. Until I started to work a full-time job, our vacation consisted of staying at my aunt and uncle's house in Ohio with my cousins for a month during summer break. It was so much fun because they were around my age, and we had a good time. Even if it wasn't a "real" vacation, I treasured that time.

This defined me as I grew up. As a child, you never think about the future and what it means to be without your father. He was not at my milestone birthdays when I turned 13, 16, 18. He wasn't there when I started my first job at 16. He didn't teach me how to drive. Nor was he there for graduation or to help me decide what the heck to do with my life afterwards. And of course, he was not there to walk me down the aisle when I got married. To this day, when I am at a wedding and hear the song "Daddy's Little Girl," I get misty-eyed and imagine that dance we were denied.

That one night in 1974 completely redefined our lives. My mother had to go to work and take care of everything. She tried to do as much with us as possible, but she was stretched thin. I know there were nights she probably cried in bed wondering how she was going to keep it all together and take care of her girls. She must have cried for the memories she would never get to make with Bob, the love of her life.

My sister was changed because she grew up only hearing the memories of my dad from the stories we would tell over the years. She never experienced the fun-loving family of four that I had for those 18 months.

As I grew into adulthood, I became increasingly self-conscious. My mother was critical of me, and I didn't have my dad to balance it out. I will never know how different I could have been growing up if he was around. This affected me all through school, so much so that I was voted the quietest girl in my senior class. I never opened my mouth at all and just faded into the background. I struggled with not thinking I was good enough. I struggled because I thought I was not pretty enough, and my clothes were not new and fashionable. I can remember getting a new winter coat and although I was tiny, it would be a large or extra-large size so I could "grow" into it and not need a new one for a few years.

Money was always an issue all my life. All of this was because of losing my dad at such an important part of my youth when I was developing who I was and what I could do.

It wasn't until years later that I realized, because of my dad's passing, I was strong enough to survive anything that came my way. And I did, alone. There was no way I could ever burden my mother with anything else while she was trying to be both parents to us. My sister was younger and always needed extra attention, I grew up fast and learned to solve my problems on my own.

As I write this chapter, I realize the impact of losing my father still has on us. My mother is quickly leaving us day by day. Her mind is being taken away by dementia. She can no longer talk about the fun times and the memories of my dad. There is no one in my family to talk about those memories. Most of the time, she doesn't even remember his name and has to ask me, when she remembers that I am her daughter.

Soon my mother will be together with her husband. He should have been here all those years we struggled, and I wish he was here now to help my sister and me, to tell us what to do. He left us before I could even say goodbye. For years I struggled with guilt, thinking if I just would have yelled for my mother when he was making those strange sounds she would have come downstairs sooner, and he may still be here with us. *I should have done something, and I let my family down.*

But I was just a child. There was nothing I could have done to change the outcome of that terrible night. God has plans for all of us, and his plan was to take my father. I thank God every day that, while it was so sudden and fast, my dad did not suffer and left when he was doing something he loved, being with his family.

I don't know what the future holds, but I do know that my sister and I will be fine. I am a survivor, and I could never have gotten through all these years without him as my guardian angel. I strongly feel he is keeping an eye on me and trying to steer me in the right direction and keep me out of trouble. When I go to his gravesite, I don't feel that he is there, even though I know physically he lies there. I feel, no, I *know* he is with me wherever I am. He is here with me right now while I write this chapter. He will be with me when I close my eyes tonight and try to go to sleep. He will be with me tomorrow morning when I open my eyes, God willing.

What have I learned over the past decades since the night that changed my life? I learned not to take life for granted. I learned how to be a strong woman from watching my mother. I learned that life is uncertain, and we must be ready for the good and the bad.

And I have learned you are never truly ready for the bad because it creeps up on you when you least expect it, and it can be unimaginable.

I have made it my mission to help empower people, especially other women. Knowledge is truly power, and I am continuously reading and learning more, professionally and personally. This is what changed me. No one helped me change from being the quiet girl that no one paid attention to; I did it myself!

I changed my appearance when I started to work full-time. I started to become more confident in my appearance when I would go out dancing with friends, and people would notice me. I got asked out on dates and eventually got married. I no longer believed that I was inferior, as I had when I was younger. I earned my bachelor's degree by working a full-time job and going to school at night with the help of my company's tuition reimbursement. Later in life, I went back to school to earn my master's degree. I joined Toastmasters to become more confident in speaking in front of people and did it even though, in the beginning, it made me sick to my stomach.

I kept pushing and pushing myself out of my comfort zone to the point of having my own TV show helping to empower others. Talk about scary! I was putting myself out there for everyone to judge. But I did it. I played the hand that was dealt to me in the game of life that terrible night, and I am still in the game.

Don't worry about me, Daddy, your baby girl Sam will be okay and will keep making you proud.

Ever since being named "The Quietest Girl" in her senior class, Denise Ann Galloni has focused on using her voice and helping others find theirs. Working with organizations and individuals through her company, DG Training Solutions, Inc., Denise has delivered over 500 presentations and keynotes to countless professionals who want to be better communicators and better leaders.

Denise's passion for leadership, communication, and corporate training has earned her a multitude of awards and recognition, including being a two-time distinguished Toastmaster and receiving the Business Choice Award for Corporate Training at the Pittsburgh Business Show.

She is the host of the award-winning TV show *Empowering You*, and she has been a featured guest on several domestic and international podcasts as well as seen in 100+ media outlets.

Denise is the author of the book, Find Your VOICE: 5 Keys to Lead and Empower Others.

To learn more about Denise Ann Galloni, please visit DeniseAnnGalloni.com.

Finding Freedom in Exactly Who I Am

By Priscilla Green

There are so many motivational quotes out there that tell us that we can in fact have our cake and eat it too. That we were made for more, that we are built for the impossible.

As a business owner, I spent too long sitting at my desk not feeling like I was having my cake or eating it. I wanted more for me and for my family. I was good at what I was doing in my business and how I was serving my clients, but I wanted more. I thought that the "more" would only ever be a dream.

Let me back up just a little for some context.

I had been working for a local business owner as an office assistant and personal assistant. I enjoyed it a lot. I had a desk in an office, I loved the variety of work, and I adored the people I worked with. My kids were involved in sports and activities and many times, I just couldn't be there because I had to be in the office for work. I felt so much guilt when the kids would come home and tell me how great they did because I missed it. I felt like I wasn't fully showing up for my kids the way they needed me to.

For years, I said that I wanted to be like the moms who were doing their own thing, able to attend all their kids' activities and functions. But I never had a job that allowed me to do so.

I saw people online talking about virtual assistance—this world of people helping others with tasks or jobs or projects, all done online—no brick-and-mortar buildings, no time clocks to punch, no rush hour commutes. To say I was intrigued is an understatement... I needed to know more.

So, I researched and dreamt of the possibilities.

I was hesitant to even try this new option that would allow me to work from home, be my own boss, and earn money because I just wasn't sure I could succeed. I had tried a lot of things before that I thought would be a smashing success, but they weren't, so I was left feeling defeated and embarrassed.

I didn't want to feel like I let anyone—especially myself—down again.

But I found myself talking about it more often. I mentioned it to my husband, and he was hesitant because he thought it might be yet another try at a sales business or MLM that wouldn't pan out.

One day, my friend Jen reached out to tell me that someone she knew was looking for a virtual assistant. Jen asked if I wanted her to pass along my name and contact information. I wasn't quite prepared, but I knew that if I didn't take the chance, the answer would be "no." This was my chance to possibly start my dream life and business. When Jen's contact chose me, I was ready. This was my chance! That was the beginning of what is now Freedom to Focus Business Support LLC.

A few months later, I was still working my day job, while doing virtual assistance on the side before work, during my lunch break, after work, etc. Then, I had more ladies reaching out to me about my services, and I was both elated and terrified. I didn't even have a real plan. I was flying by the seat of my pants, and it was both terrifying and exhilarating. Here I was, working my own business, and people were signing on and paying me to work with them!

It wasn't all perfect, though. One issue I had was that I didn't realize I shouldn't just take on anyone and everyone who came to me looking for help. I didn't have the clarity and boundaries that are needed to build a strong foundation. Looking back now, I see it so clearly, but as I started out, I didn't see it. While I wanted so badly to succeed at this business and build my dream life, taking on just anyone was not the answer. That would not allow me to truly build my business, and it would quickly cause me to burn out and add stress to my life.

I added more clients, the work was increasing, and I thought that maybe just maybe I could handle leaving my job... but that would mean quitting the stability and comfort of my full-time job.

Could I *really* do that? What if I lost clients? What if I actually didn't have what it takes to succeed?

What if, what if, what if.

Yes, I had clients at this point. Yes, the workload was increasing. Yes, I was doing a good job and loving it.

So, what was the problem? What was holding me back?

I talked to my husband, and he said, "You can do this. You *are* doing it. You will do amazing at it. You just need to go for it." Was this man crazy? How in the world could he believe in me when *I* didn't fully believe in me? How was it that he could he see this and I couldn't? I felt so loved and supported in that moment. I truly had someone who saw the magic in me that I hadn't. I had a rush of calm and determination come over me, and for the first time, I thought it was a real possibility.

And while I thought he was nuts for encouraging me to quit my job and build this crazy dream of mine, it was that conversation that really got me started on this journey of what was ahead for me.

I was in several Facebook groups for virtual assistants and online service providers. There were so many resources out there that gave me guidance on what I needed to do to move forward. I would read others' success stories, and that pang of jealousy, urgency, and wanting to be where they were made me realize that I could do the same thing that they were doing. And while I didn't feel the confidence that I saw in others, I wanted it badly enough that I knew that if I worked hard, learned more, and worked on myself, I had what I needed to move forward with growing and building that dream life and business.

My hours at work had decreased, and I was working more hours in my business, so I decided that it was time to give notice to my boss that I was quitting. I wrote my resignation letter so many times. I was sick to my stomach at the thought of hitting send. Who was I? What the hell was I doing?

I was going off on my own, away from the comfort and stability of my job. I was going to build this life and business of my dreams so I could finally be there for my kids and family and live life on my own terms.

Not too long after going full-time in my business, I started growing even more. I had plenty of clients, so I had already replaced my income from my job. I was doing this! I was networking more, getting my name out there, and receiving a bunch of referrals from current clients and past clients. I was feeling confident. I was now an executive assistant to my clients, and I was doing a fantastic job.

In my own head and at my desk, I was a *bona fide* business owner. I was succeeding at the very thing that made me sick to my stomach to think about just a few months prior and making more money than I ever had before. I had arrived!!

Or had I?

Part of the life and business that I had dreamt of was being able to attend functions during the day, go to fitness classes at my friend's center, and go out to lunch when I wanted. It was the freedom that I had been seeking all along. To be my own boss and be successful.

I had checked all the boxes, but ...

One day I went to my friend's fitness center for a class and was chatting with someone I knew. She said to me, "So are you still doing your little business thing?" It was a punch to the gut. *My little business thing?!* I wasn't upset at her, and I knew that she didn't mean it to be hurtful or diminishing. I was upset that I hadn't shared with others what I had been doing and how much I had done to help my clients. Here I was making more money than I had ever made, elevating my business, and elevating myself, and yet no one even knew. No one knew because I was holding back. I wasn't sharing my brilliance with the world. I know that part of the reason why is because I was afraid.

I was afraid of being judged. I was afraid of not being taken seriously. I was upset with myself because I was allowing my fear and inner critic to hold me back.

And so, I drew a line in the sand.

I wanted to make sure that I was taking advantage of different opportunities where I could meet other women business owners who could potentially be my client. I joined groups where I could learn more, offer my expertise to help others, and show up as an expert in my field. I started doing some interviews, I even presented for a huge summit with thousands of attendees. And I was interviewed on a podcast. I felt like I was on top of the world! I was being seen, and I was being heard as an expert and a leader, for the first time. It was exhilarating, and I gained so much self-confidence from those experiences.

But as many business owners will tell you, with those amazing highs come some lows. There are so many quotes about how, when you fall, you need to get back up, or that you just have to keep pushing, or other things that are supposed to motivate, but in those moments, sometimes, it is really hard to push through and forget those lows.

The lows did follow that period when I felt like I was floating in the clouds from finally being seen and heard as a legit, successful business owner. I focused so much on imposed income levels that people post. Since I thought I had to make $10,000 a month to be truly successful and be taken seriously, I was stressed out, overwhelmed, and rundown because I was focused on the wrong thing. I was not taking the time to work on myself and show myself love and gratitude for what I had built.

I began working with a coach, and it was amazing. One of the things she suggested was to stop focusing on that income goal. The stress it caused did nothing positive for me or my business. That coaching program gave me so many *aha* moments and solid foundations for me and my business that I was able to relax, allow things to flow more easily, and feel more aligned with my goals.

And after only one month of focusing on me, I hit that $10k a month income goal!

Another piece of advice I was given was to build a team for my business, so I hired four team members who would allow me some time freedom to better serve my clients. The best part was that I was empowering other women to use their skills and their expertise to build the life of their dreams. I wanted to make sure I was working with integrity and being a true leader. I wanted to do for my team members what other women have done for me.

So, I helped teach them, I listened to their input, and I worked with them to make sure I was fully utilizing their skills and their experience. In that way, I was truly able to show up as a leader, not only for my team but also for other business owners I was networking with to show them what is possible and how to build a great culture within your company.

I started feeling more comfortable in my skin as a person and as a business owner. I was finally able to feel like I was shining in my own brilliance, and at the same time, I was showing love to my clients and my clients' clients. What I wanted more than anything was to build real relationships with women business owners to be sure that they felt fully supported. And that was exactly what I was doing. I stopped taking on just anyone as a client and started refining my business to realize who I wanted to work with—six-, seven-, and eight-figure women business owners—and how. I wanted to work more intimately with these women and truly help them with their businesses.

I was no longer just checking items off a task list; I was helping to strategize, brainstorm, and give suggestions for the systems and processes in their businesses.

It took a long time and a lot of ups and downs for me to realize that my true magic was these amazing relationships that I built with other women business owners. I was helping them in their businesses and allowing them the freedom of time to fully serve their clients and shine in *their* own brilliance. I finally felt so comfortable in my skin and in my expertise, and it was time to build upon that.

It was time to grow again.

I knew that if I wanted to truly grow in my expertise and in my skill set, I had more learning to do, so I decided to become an accredited online business manager to learn how to take on more of a leadership role and become a partner to business owners rather than just handling general administrative tasks. I enrolled in an accredited course to learn several skill sets. I completed that course and passed all the course requirements to become accredited.

This helped me with my self-confidence even more and really allowed me to see the levels that I could reach in helping women grow their businesses. In doing so, I reached income goals that I had set for myself that I did not think I would ever reach.

If you had told me earlier that I would reach my prior yearly income at my previous job within a two-month span in my business, I would have laughed and told you that you were a dreamer! But it was true, and as I looked in amazement at my income, tears also started to fall because I was so grateful for this life and this business that I had built through so many ups and downs, fears and doubts, frustration, and stress, it was something that I thought I could only dream of.

So here I am, almost five years after leaving my full-time job to go full-time in my business. I knew it would not be easy, and I knew there would be a lot of ups and downs, but there was so much that I did not know. I did not know that I could even gain the confidence that I gained over those years. I did not know that I would come out from the shadows of my former self to proclaim that I am a legit and successful business owner and that I am living my life on my terms. I never knew that I would become aware of and be okay with who I really am, my true self. I am no longer just someone's assistant, or someone's wife, or someone's mother—I am me, and I am brilliant, smart, funny, loving, caring, encouraging, supportive, and so many other things.

There is a process that business owners go through that is lovingly referred to as the "messy middle," and sometimes we feel that we've made it through that messy middle only to return there again a time or two or maybe even three.

But I promise you that it is worth it, because in that messy middle there are lessons to be learned about how to move forward, how to persevere, and about just how truly powerful you are.

I have no regrets about the journey other than wishing that I had the confidence to do it sooner. I only wish that I had as much faith in myself as my husband did the day he told me that I had it within me to fully jump into this business. I am forever grateful to my husband for believing in me before I did. He has continued to be my sounding board, my encouragement, and the person to calm me down when I want to burn it all down.

So if you are ready to take that leap of faith, just know that you have that magic within you. You are enough, and you are smart and able to take what you can only dream of and make it your reality. It may take some time for you to really learn about yourself and know who you are to build up your confidence, but you should always bet on yourself.

I know that there is so much more of the story to be written as I continue in my business. I cannot wait to see what lies ahead for me, for my family, for my clients, and for my team.

Priscilla is the owner and CEO of Freedom to Focus Business Support LLC. She works with six-, seven-, and eight-figure women business owners as an online business manager and agency owner. She prides herself on working in full integrity and creating genuine relationships with her clients. For more information, please visit freedomtofocusbusinesssupport.net.

Priscilla can be found on social media:

Facebook: www.facebook.com/FreedomtoFocus

Instagram: www.instagram.com/freedomtofocus

Creating and Embracing my Dear Friend's Legacy

By Darlene Barruso Kruth

To say that my college career was unique would be an understatement. Twenty-year-olds aren't supposed to lose one of their best friends. Reflecting back on it now, 37 years later, I can certainly say that I received an education for life that has helped me unleash my soul-level magic, which is centered on helping others.

I grew up believing I would go to college, get a good education, and study a subject that would result in landing me a good-paying, stable job. I wanted to be independent and support myself. I was told that my college years would be the best four years of my young life. I was happy—especially when I learned that I wouldn't be alone on The Bluff (Duquesne University's campus nickname), as several of my high school friends would be joining me there.

In August 1983, filled with excitement and anxiety, I began my college career studying accounting at Duquesne University in Pittsburgh, Pa. Little did I know, much of my education would not come from textbooks and lectures, but from the experiences I had outside the classroom.

Thanks to the enthusiasm of our group leaders, Mary Sherwood and Ron Corey, the first session with our freshmen orientation group didn't disappoint. It was on this day that I met four classmates: Liz Leila Acevedo (she would be my roommate for the next three years), Lee Marie Carruthers, Ken Autieri, and Tom Bartolec. All would become life-long friends.

While Liz was enrolled in the pharmacy program, the other four of us were all enrolled in the business school and quickly realized we would have several classes together in our first semester. Our group of friends had two priorities. The first was avoiding the climb up "Cardiac Hill" from Rockwell Hall more than once a day, unless we were taking a night class. Our other priority was to avoid scheduling classes between 3 and 4 pm so we could all race back to the dorms to watch either *Guiding Light* or *General Hospital*. Yes, even the guys were hooked!

For our sophomore year, Lee transferred to New York, closer to home, as she wanted to be near a beach, and I had suggested that she not swim in any of Pittsburgh's three rivers. I'm forever grateful that the one year we spent with Lee was more than enough for us to create a lasting friendship, and we still keep in touch regularly. I went to her surprise 21st birthday party, and we even have a healthy rivalry when her NY Jets play my Pittsburgh Steelers.

Liz, Ken, and Tom all survived pledging and joined a social sorority (Alpha Phi) and a social fraternity (Gamma Phi, "Gammas"); I instead chose to get involved with the Student Government Association and the Union Program Board.

Tom and I became orientation group leaders and helped with the dance marathon to raise money for muscular dystrophy. Tom became a Eucharistic minister with Campus Ministry and a resident assistant in the St. Martin's Living Learning Center dorm. My active involvement on campus led me to positions on Dean Glen Beeson's student advisory board for the school of business, and as an ambassador to the university president, Father Donald S. Nesti, C. S. Sp., I attended events, both on and off campus, either with Father Nesti or as his representative.

Even with all these activities, I would go home every weekend to work a part-time job, which helped me pay for books and the late-night pizzas for study sessions. My absence from campus on weekends left my friends to their own demise, which could be the subject of a whole other book!

Life was good.

Fast forward to junior year, December 1985. On Sunday, December 8th, Tom and I were studying together for a test. We talked about our holiday plans and the fact that that day was the five-year anniversary of John Lennon's death. We commented that his life had been taken far too soon. Little did I know how, within the next 24 hours, that discussion would take on an entirely new meaning.

The next day, our test was at 2:15 pm in Rockwell Hall. Tom was struggling, the last one to finish, so I waited for him in front of the classroom alongside the professor. As we walked back to the dorms around 3:15 pm, he said he had a slight headache and said he was going to lie down before dinner, but instead, he came out to watch the Gammas play street hockey. When the other team didn't have enough players, they canceled the organized game. It became a pick-up game, which means anyone could play, and Tom decided to play.

I had just wandered down to the front of the dorms to check in on the game before dinner. I had no idea Tom had collapsed in the middle of the game. Paramedics were called, they administered CPR, and he was taken by ambulance to Mercy Hospital, right next to campus.

Tom was pronounced dead at the hospital a short time later. When the call came in to a friend's dorm room where we were all gathered waiting for news, feelings of disbelief overwhelmed all of us... crying, screaming, distraught, especially the guys who were out on the hockey court who saw him collapse.

We all struggled tremendously with the loss and lack of closure; there was no viewing or formal funeral in Pittsburgh, just endless days spent in the university chapel attending organized services and sitting quietly with each other and sharing our memories of Tom. The administration kept a close eye on my classmates and me since most of us were away from home and had not suffered this type of loss before. Only a few people were able to make the trip to Delaware, where Tom was from, for the memorial service; I was not. Months later I vaguely remember learning that the autopsy report was somewhat inconclusive, but referenced scar tissue around Tom's heart that most likely resulted from an infection he had as a child.

Recently, Dr. James Fitzpatrick, the dean of students and the Gamma's faculty advisor in 1985, confided in me that his conversation with Tom's parents when they arrived on campus was one of the most difficult of his professional career. My friends and I had the opportunity to meet with Tom's parents when they visited campus, and they appreciated hearing all the stories of Tom's college antics! I think they may have already known that he wasn't a saint, especially after they found his fake ID when they cleaned out his dorm room! He was just two-and-a-half months shy of his 21st birthday when he passed away.

Even though I was only 30 minutes from home, and my parents wanted me to come home for a few days, I was determined to stay with my friends. That's where I needed to be. My parents couldn't understand the magnitude of my grief. They mentioned that I had lost people in my life who I was close to before but hadn't behaved in such a distraught manner. To put it into perspective, most of the folks I had lost up to this point in my life were much older, some suffering from illnesses, and their passing would have been imminent.

Tom's death didn't meet any of these criteria.

During the months that followed, I sometimes think that I cried my lifetime's allotment of tears. I'm very grateful for the friends who would step up and stand by me for the duration of our college careers and some to this day.

There were many sleepless nights. Often, Chris Coyne let me sit with him during his night shifts at the front desk of the St. Martin's dorm where Tom had lived. Some nights we'd spend chatting nonstop, and other times we'd sit quietly or study.

Because Tom's sudden passing was just a few days prior to the beginning of semester finals, my professors all offered to let me (and several classmates), take incompletes in our courses and tackle the finals after the holidays. I declined and persevered through all the exams so I could just put the entire semester behind me. My GPA during my junior year took a hit, but somehow I was able to right the ship; I landed a tax department internship the summer after my junior year, and subsequently a full-time auditing position upon graduation.

When I went home for the holiday break, I begrudgingly participated in all the typical holiday activities while constantly trying to hold back a nonstop cascade of tears. I told myself that I had to come up with a way to turn this tragic loss into something positive and find a way to honor Tom's legacy and the impact he'd had on the University community. Tom had been deeply involved with campus organizations and provided valuable guidance to many students.

I decided I wanted to create a scholarship in Tom's memory. At 20 years old, I was traveling way out of my comfort zone. As a presidential ambassador, my first thought was to meet with the University president, Father Nesti.

I spoke to Tom's parents and fraternity brothers to explain my intentions and to gain their support. Once they were on board, I met with Paul Stabile, the director of development, to start the process of drafting a legal document to govern administration of the funds.

We set up the criteria for application: you had to be either a sophomore or junior in the School of Business, have a minimum GPA of 3.25, have a record of community and or university service, and agree to an in-person interview with the selection committee. The selection committee would consist of me, a representative from the Student Life and Residence Life departments, a business school professor who I hand-picked (initially this was Dr. Richard Bond, a professor of economics, one of Tom's favorites), and the Gammas' current president.

I then embarked on the fundraising process to have the award endowed for perpetuity. I was, and still am, far from a polished public speaker, but I had to "embrace the suck" for the good of the cause. My grassroots effort included scheduling speeches in front of all types of campus organizations requesting donations. This was long before Facebook's Go Fund Me pages existed! I somehow juggled these activities while continuing my coursework and working two part-time jobs. Looking back on it now, it was clearly the beginning of my Super Woman syndrome!

Amid my despair and focused fundraising efforts, I also found it in my heart to make good on a Christmas gift for Tom's girlfriend Christine, because it was the right thing to do. I knew exactly what to get. I purchased two tickets to see Anthony Quinn perform his iconic role of Tevye in *Fiddler on the Roof* at the Syria Mosque in February 1986 (Tom would have turned 21 on February 28th), told her that my friend had canceled on me at the last minute, and invited her to join me. Thankfully she accepted the invitation.

It wasn't until the bus ride home that I told her the truth, that Tom was intending to buy the tickets for her as a gift, at my suggestion, the night before his passing, even though it wasn't really his cup of tea. To say that a waterfall of tears ensued for both of us at that moment would be a gross understatement! I can only imagine what the other folks on the bus that evening thought about these two young women just bawling their eyes out.

Another unexpected twist to this story occurred on the evening of the student government elections in 1986. My ballot counting was interrupted by several Gamma Phi brothers rushing in to tell me I had to leave with them. Outside, they presented me with Gamma Phi letters and told me that I had been voted into the fraternity as a little sister! The impact of this development, just two days prior to what would have been Tom's 21st birthday, was not lost on me.

I eventually chose a big brother, Drew. He brought me peanut brittle when I had my wisdom teeth extracted, and, with his bare hands, was able to remove a store sensor from a formal dress for me without damaging it, just in the nick of time before the Fraternity's 70th anniversary celebration! The Gammas are the oldest local fraternity in

Pennsylvania, and I have assisted with every anniversary celebration up to its 100th in 2016! To this day, because of our unique experiences, these Gamma Phi brothers are a tight-knit group of guys, some of whom I count among my closest friends. While I never dated any Gammas during my Duquesne years, I eventually married one of them, and we've been together for 31 years!

In the summer between my junior and senior years, I traveled to Delaware to spend some time with Tom's family and friends. The trip was important for me as I finally got to accept the reality of his passing by visiting his grave. I still visit his grave to just sit and chat with him when I'm in the area.

After spending almost a year raising scholarship funds, the Alpha Phi Delta (APD) fraternity offered to donate a portion of the proceeds from their annual Valentine's ball event in February 1987 to the cause. They asked me to attend the event to accept the donation. I asked my dear friend, Chris Coyne, the current Gamma Phi president, to join me in accepting that donation.

The APD's donation was just over $600, and it put me over the $5,000 minimum I needed to have the fund endowed. I was overwhelmed with emotion and could barely speak! After an entire year, I felt like I could finally breathe again! Several of Tom's family members' contributions, coupled with my campus efforts, resulted in the Thomas D. Bartolec Endowed Award Fund being established in spring 1987, just in time for my graduation.

The first award was granted from the interest earned in spring 1989.

To date, the fund has distributed over $36,000 in awards to deserving students in Duquesne's AJ Palumbo School of Business Administration. For many years, I have to admit, it was difficult for me to hold back tears during the applicants' interviews when they would ask about who Tom was and how the award came to be. My memories of Tom are of his smile, the bounce in his step, torn jeans (long before they were a thing), dedication to class work, willingness to help others, and his sense of humor and laugh. The Thomas D Bartolec Endowed Award is clearly his legacy for the impact he had on the university and me. And to think that it all started with my personal donation of $100.

To this day, I still make every effort to visit a church to light a candle, sit quietly, say a few prayers, talk to Tom, and thank him for his friendship on the anniversary of his passing (December 9th) and on his birthday (February 28th).

Since this first experience, I have been asked to assist with the creation, administration, and distribution of several other scholarships and awards. I now serve on seven different boards or organization scholarship administration/selection committees that distribute between $200,000 and $300,000 in funds to qualified and deserving high school and college students annually.

Because I feel driven to give back even more, I've recently decided to work toward creating a new scholarship focusing on entrepreneurship at Washington & Jefferson College. This is to honor the memory of a real estate colleague and dear friend, Danny Gillette, who passed away suddenly in October 2021. I've also been asked to spearhead the creation of two other scholarship programs in 2023 on behalf of other organizations.

At times, this work can feel overwhelming, both emotionally and from a time commitment perspective. But in my heart, I often feel like I'm doing the work with my friend Tom sitting right beside me.

Every experience in your life leaves its mark. I discovered a true passion for this volunteer work that I believe would not have ever come to light had it not been for the tragic loss I suffered. For that, I will be forever grateful. I miss Tom and know he is watching over me, his family, and Gamma brothers. To quote a lyric from Wiz Khalifa's song "See You Again," "It's been a long day without you my friend. / I'll tell you all about it when I see you again."[1]

While this story began over 37 years ago, it continues to evolve to this day. 2023 may be the year I finally turn this passion into a viable business. I'm eternally thankful to all those who have supported me in my efforts to continually

---

1 Wiz Khalifa, ft. Charlie Puth, "See You Again," track #10 on *Most Wanted, Vol. 2*, 2015.

unleash my soul-level magic, and those who have entrusted me with honoring the legacy of their loved ones and businesses by doing something I truly love.

Darlene Barruso Kruth, a native Pittsburgher, started her professional career as a certified public accountant and is now a multi-million dollar producing real estate agent with Berkshire Hathaway HomeServices The Preferred Realty. A published author, she writes quarterly real estate industry insight articles for two local *InCommunity* magazines.

Darlene married her husband Frank, also a Gamma, in 1995; enjoys cooking and entertaining family, friends, colleagues, and networking partners; and supports Pittsburgh's cultural arts and sports teams.

Little did Darlene know that her creative efforts to preserve a legacy after the sudden passing of a college classmate would result in a lifelong passion to help others. Since 1986, her volunteer side hustle has been to create, administer, and distribute scholarship and award funds to deserving local high school and Duquesne University's AJ Palumbo School of Business Administration students. She even has three new scholarship programs in the works for 2023: one for students studying entrepreneurship at Washington & Jefferson College in memory of a dear friend and fellow real estate colleague, one in memory of a Peters Twp. business owner to benefit residents of the Washington City Mission, and one for the Pittsburgh Elevated & Emerging Leaders (PEEL) organization.

Darlene currently serves on the following scholarship and award boards/selection committees:

- Thomas D. Bartolec Endowed Award: benefitting Duquesne University AJ Palumbo School of Business Administration students.
- Duquesne University AJ Palumbo School of Business Administration Scholarship committee—oversees 11 scholarships/awards
- Duquesne University Women's Advisory Board: Mary Pappert School of Music Scholarship
- Berkshire Hathaway HomeServices The Preferred Realty: Dream, Innovate & Grow Scholarships
- Patti & Walter Blenko Scholarship Fund for the Performing or Technical Arts
- Lawrence H. Kruth Memorial Scholarship at South Fayette Township High School
- Rotary Club of Pleasant Hills scholarships

For more info on applications for any of these scholarship funds, Darlene may be contacted at dbkruthrealtor@gmail.com.

For more info on Darlene's real estate services in the Pittsburgh, Pa., area or worldwide, please contact her via email at dkruth@TPRSold.com, on Facebook (Darlene Kruth, Realtor, or Darlene Kruth), or on LinkedIn (Darlene Kruth).

My New Normal: What I was Born to Do

By Amanda Kunkel

"You know you're psychic, right?" she purred in her well-trained Hollywood voice.

Her piercing blue eyes stared into me, seeing the "me" that no one else could. She waited for my response.

Celebrities from Hollywood can be terrifying in their gazes, trained for the camera and all, I thought.

My mind raced with all kinds of answers; my heart sped up, beating so fast it pushed beads of sweat down my forehead and onto my face.

"Of course you're psychic," she continued. "I'm going to train you, OK?"

This was the moment that set everything in motion—and changed the course of my life, forever.

By the time I was in my early 20s, I had been entirely on my own for years. I had no family to care for me, feed me, or shelter me. The panic and anxiety attacks over food and rent had been relentless—so much so that I channeled all my energy into making a life where I knew I would always have food and shelter.

In doing this, I had accidentally crafted a house of cards: I made myself believe that all I had to do was make it through grad school and I would be set for life. What really happened was that I had built and planned a life based on fear, but I didn't really know I was stuck at this point.

So when this woman asked if I knew I was psychic, I immediately thought *no*—after all, saying *yes* would topple my house of cards. Admitting to another desire within myself would collapse my safe space.

Everything I THOUGHT I wanted as a career and in life up until then was wrong.

I *knew* I was psychic. I spent my upbringing playing with angels, seeing dead people, and having prophetic dreams. Knowing things I shouldn't have known about adults. Yet I ignored my gift when I needed it the most: being on my own at 17. I thought that the "logical" next steps (get a full-time job, go to university) would create food and shelter.

So I took a deep breath and said, "sure."

I could feel the mundaneness of simply grabbing coffee, scrambling to make it to class on time, and attempting to make new friends slip away. It was as if the sun finally came out after the darkest of days.

Several months later, it had become the norm for me to leave my psychology class, drive three hours, and help the Catholic Church perform house exorcisms.

That was my new normal!

In fact, the class I was taking that semester was Abnormal Psychology... what I was doing in my own psychic work was abnormal too! So I wasn't off, per se, in my course choices.

Before the exorcisms, though, my psychic mentor and I met on the telephone (landline days) and over email. She walked me through my first tarot readings, taught me how to open up my senses, and helped me clear some of the crap that had been holding me back from going deep into my soul.

I doubted myself a lot. Even though my soul was leading me to what it KNEW was the right path. My University advisor tried to talk me out of it all the time. I was pushing boundaries that made other people uncomfortable because I was not following the "normal" route. My honors college paper on telekinesis barely passed with a D. Why? Well the subject matter wasn't "in line" with University standards. On top of that, my friends either thought I was doing the coolest thing ever, or that I was crazy. I have lost many "friends" over the years when they learned what I do and how I do it. I've had to leave behind so much to stay on this soul-led path. It was and IS painful, still. But I learned to see the opening of what the next chapter could bring and focus on the good there.

I got to do "cool things," like read for the psychic's celebrity friends and assist her on police cold cases of missing persons.

The house exorcisms were a bonus from a paranormal group I had been with in college. Just as I was opening my heart to allowing in my psychic senses, this paranormal group got a message from a homeowner, who had been directed to email the group by the archbishop.

I can't share details about that specific experience because of NDAs, but what I can share was that it was a period of intense expansion.

The more I went within myself and touched the hearts and lives of people through my psychic gifts, the more I fell out of love with grad school.

Deep down, I knew I was meant to do more than sit in a room or a lab and let people talk about their issues but not DO anything about those issues. Yes, I said it: psychotherapists don't really provide the container for MOVEMENT. They DO provide containers for slow internal shifting, which is fabulous for some people. However, I am a results-oriented person who loves speed. When we take the whole mind, body, and soul into account, we can end up seeing powerful, fast results, which is something psychotherapy does not do.

One way that psychics might work is in "attack" mode to combat evil, and that is what you see in the movies. But I work with love and light only. I knew that this type of "spiritual warfare" was not for me. The only reason I was there was that my energy held The Light. I brought LOVE into the house. To the family.

I never experienced any extreme scenarios, like a person vomiting split pea soup while their head turned in circles! That is a tiny part of what could take place. When you're in that space, you know something is wrong because there is an ABSENCE of love. Like all the love that was once present was sucked out of the home and nothing is left there. (Which is different from no love having been there ever.) That is how the experience is 90% of the time and what it DOES to the heart, soul, and mind of the family in the house. When an entity is actively coming into a home, the feeling is entirely different. And again when it purposely "attacks." Neither of which is my field of expertise (nor were they).

I could bring a flood of love and light into a space where mass trauma happened because both love and trauma had built the hope that got me through my first 17 years. While I was nervous about the exorcisms, I was never really scared. I could literally feel the love emanating from my body and protecting everyone in that space. This love led me to the next eight years of deep diving with angels and God and opening up to being loved myself.

I knew getting my Ph.D. in psychology was not going to let me use these gifts. I already had gotten into arguments with my advisors over research topics dealing with the heart and soul. "It's just not done" was the answer.

Even though I took the GREs (grad school admissions tests) and did the grad school tour... it ultimately wasn't in my heart.

I couldn't do it.

I had completely changed.

I finally felt like ME.

I hadn't been thinking then about "the money I could make" as a business owner when I was thinking about the next steps in my career. I only knew I wanted to positively impact lives with my gifts.

I could no longer be the scared teenager that society had made. But a powerhouse of a woman who knew where her soul fit in this world.

Today in my business, I connect high-achieving businesswomen with The Universe (God, Goddess, etc.) to receive their direct steps to multiple six- and seven-figure revenues... a far cry from slinging tarot cards and participating in house exorcisms.

I didn't always talk about the work that I did as I grew my gifts. I often kept it a secret, wanting to bury the heavy energy and not answer questions about it. With the rise of "ghost hunting" TV programs, the whole world seemed to be sucking up as much as they could about the paranormal, so I knew people would be curious about the work I was doing.

But what I did wasn't something glamorous. To be talked about and gawked at. So I hid. I wasn't sure HOW to talk about what I did and definitely didn't want to "put it on display." It took me a while to integrate this part of myself and fully own this part of my development.

The more I deepened my relationship with God, and my skill set grew, the more I felt comfortable about the work I had done. I had been doubting my own abilities because... I was so young. I am not Catholic. The people around me (friends and family) thought I was a bit bonkers when I told them about my work with the Catholic Church. So I really had to go within. Find me. My beliefs and strengths. So I felt my own power. And really KNEW to the core that I was a whole, healthy, and powerful woman. That I wouldn't ever put myself in actual harm's way and my sanity was more than intact.

I remember meeting renowned demonologist John Zaffis in 2007. He said, "Oh, YOU are Amanda," which took me by surprise. (That and a friend had just bumped into me and spilled coffee all over my white dress...)

How did this person know who l was? Well, that's a story for another time. However, he looked right at me and said, "Don't think for one second that you were crazy. You were not. You are not. You were one of the sanest and most protected people." In the proceeding conversation with him, everything clicked. Something in my psyche allowed this wise father figure to give me permission to OWN what I knew to be true about my history. My experience and myself.

After this, very slowly, I started talking about my experiences with fellow woo-woo people. Which led to me slowly opening up more to the general public.

I still don't wear a T-shirt talking about my time with the Catholic Church. Due to pop culture, there is so much fear, and false information is spread. I won't add to it. But I am happy to explain my history and WHY I have discernment—that I can see the larger picture of anything as it relates to the unending time of The Universe.

You are either born with it or you are not. While you can practice this skill, the true depth of *knowing you have it* is simply part of you or not.

It was the integration of ALL parts of me (the past, my current state) and the personal plus professional work I did that really allowed me to shine as a business leader.

At 40 years old, the divine mixture of my business career (I worked full time through the first part of college), my psych degree, and my psychic abilities (plus that spiritual warfare) all culminated in what I do today.

I make millionaires out of women business owners (true fact).

I do this by helping women tune into their unique skills. Their hearts. Allowing all who they BE to shine. So they don't have to be those masks society created.

My own journey echoes exactly what I do for others now.

And it is WHY I can "hold and not drop" powerhouse CEOs.

I'm not holding them to standards. I'm holding them in an etheric container, gridded with the webbing of The Universe, almost like a cocoon. That "cocoon" is unique for each woman. This is where she transforms and shifts into her desired reality. I hold that and everything that gets shaken up outside of that container—when you get closer to who you are meant to be, it disrupts everything. For example, people were benefitting from you staying who you were and not achieving your next big goal, so they will push against the change. And no matter what I see, I don't run. I've had people tell me deep secrets of pain and darkness from their lives, and none of it phases me. I hold the container with The Universe and hold that vision of their desired self firm.

The "serious three-piece business suit" women seek me out because my reputation in this area precedes me. They know I won't back down, won't buck at their shit or judge them. But will hold them to their highest and best good. With no way in hell of dropping them. Because for me, this is the easiest and most graceful part of all the work I have done.

This work gives them permission for not just shelter and food (without panic attacks or hustle) but the deepest acceptance that we can all live lives of luxury, adventure, and FUN. Where we allow all those freak flag parts of ourselves to shine.

Life is one big reflection. The things that created and molded me were the light against the dark. (I mean come on, most 24-year-olds can't do house exorcisms with the Catholic Church.) In my life now, I allow the light (good) and dark (not so sparkly) parts of myself to mix and synthesize. Allowing love to always win. Leading with my heart even when my brain tells me something doesn't logically make sense.

The best things in life do not logically make sense. They are welcomed by the heart and spirit with trust and faith. There, that is where magic unfolds. Where The Universe works beyond what the mind can imagine. Trust. Lean in. Open your heart.

Looking back, there is ZERO way I could have seen my life unfold like this. Even with my gifts. It was not an easy path. Yet I LOVE all the depths and all parts of myself. It's what allows me to touch so many lives and have an impact in the world. That, I am thankful for.

Amanda Kunkel assists radical self-thinking businesswomen who have demonstrated business maturity and the ambition for acceleration. They are ready to embark on a dimensional energy shift away from doing into BEING. They hear their spirit calling loud and clear to step into their Elite Empress self.

With her Psychic SuperPower, Amanda conveys to women their unique Universe Map, which is THE WAY to stepping into 7 figures. They created this map with The Universe before they were born. The paradigm shift already exists within them.

As a lifetime psychic with decades of professional experience, Amanda's skills are the SuperPower that allow women to shift from Income Generating to Wealth BE-ING.

Amanda provides game-changing opportunities for women to step into true, deep leadership in her industry, based on radical self-thinking and new paradigms.

Amanda will walk with women as they move into 7 figures and beyond.

- Shifting into new dimensional BEING
- Breaking free from current groups and programs that have been limiting their thinking and energy
- Stepping away from the norm to allow their thinking to move them into millions (and out of the "approved" way of waiting your turn at it)
- Stepping out of her old shell and space as *The Universe Unfolds Through Her*

Connect with Amanda:

Website: https://www.amandakunkel.com/

Facebook group:
https://www.facebook.com/groups/LaserPointYourBusinessWithTheUniverse/

Facebook:
https://www.facebook.com/AmandaKunkel4444

Heartbreak and a Radical Change

By Marta Mazzoni

"If you are unhappy, move. You are not a tree."

~ Unknown

Was there ever a time when you felt you had your whole life planned out, but then life threw you a curveball? Heartbreak is a powerful catalyst. The dissolution of a relationship can derail you. Love blinds us to the things we don't want to look at—at least it did for me.

It was the beginning of summer 2004. I was blissfully in love—the kind where you lose who you are, forget your friends, and drop all your plans except the ones that revolve around that person. It was not healthy. I ignored the warning signs; the flame was burning so bright, and all I wanted to do was keep it going.

My then-boyfriend of three years informed me that he took a job in New Jersey. He had mentioned it months before, but with my rose-colored glasses on, I had been in complete denial that it would happen. My heart sank. It was the first time I felt true grief. We had all the conversations about long-distance relationships, visits, new furniture, and experiences. For years we had planned on moving in together, jobs, marriage, kids.

In a single phone call, my world was shaken like a snow globe. I couldn't stop it.

I am a planner at heart. I'd had our life mapped out. In the weeks following that conversation, I would find myself with the usual grief that comes when you lose something you love so much: Anxiety, despair, denial. I cried myself to sleep.

The idea of feeling this way forever paralyzed me. I pictured my life without him, and it looked empty. I had lost... *me*. How was I going to meet myself again? I had no clue. I was overcome with a sense of hopelessness and resigned myself to my life as it was.

The weeks ticked by. Jeremy[2] moved. We continued to talk as if we were together. I was living at my parent's house, the last of my siblings to be there. One sleepless night, I found myself in my sister Nina's old bedroom at 2 am.

My only true escape then was the internet. It was new and exciting, and with my AOL handle and various chat rooms, it was a refuge for my grief. Then something stirred inside me. I felt inspired by these online strangers from around the world. Their stories and shared experiences made me not feel so alone.

---

2 This name has been changed to maintain confidentiality.

Then I remembered a dream I'd had before I'd fallen head-over-heels for cute a boy in a band. I remembered what I wanted to be.

Growing up as the baby of the family in the suburbs of Pittsburgh, Pa., with hardly any neighbors or friends to play with, my siblings Nina and Deni would create these incredibly long scavenger hunts to keep me occupied. These distractions would last for days, and they were EPIC! Clues led to more clues. It all kept me busy and out of their hair.

These treasure hunts molded me into the person I am today. No matter what happens, I know I can always come back to this voracious curiosity about the world around me, and a need to explore.

As I sat in my sister's room that night, that memory crept through me. I typed "archeology," "history," "work," and "Italy" into the search engine, and pored over the results. I landed on a page that piqued my interest—in Italian, it read: *Tomb excavation volunteer project in southern Sicily*.

A tomb excavation? How incredible! I had studied archaeology in college, yet still immediately assumed that there was no way it would be available to me. I kept reading...

A museum in Agrigento is using the aid of a small nonprofit company composed of students and volunteers to help it rebuild. Kalat is offering a small number of open positions this summer for volunteers to help dig up old tombs and artifacts. Cost: 350 euros for three weeks, including room and board.

There was a number attached for information. I immediately picked up our landline and figured out how to dial Italy. A sleepy woman answered "*Pronto?*"

Oh shit, I thought. I am talking to a human being on the other side of the world who doesn't even speak English!

I stumbled through my intermediate Italian, apologizing profusely, and somehow understood that she would send information to my email the next day.

A bit of a backstory about my travels up to this point: there had been virtually none. I once visited my sister in Vegas for a month and flew to see her. It was a terrible experience. Turbulence, a storm, and they aired *Titanic*. I had many panic attacks and attached myself to a bald lawyer named Sam for the duration of the trip.

I learned that I was terrified to fly. To get to Italy, I'd need to take three planes and a two-tiered bus ride for three hours.

Oh god.

Then something extremely interesting happened: I split myself into two people. These two Martas were having a frank discussion.

Marta One: This... crazy adventure I found? A flight of fancy that will pass. It could be a scam!

Marta Two: It isn't a scam. Did you not just call and wake up a poor, random lady in the middle of the night and embarrass yourself? That wasn't me, that was ALL YOU. You did that. You picked up the phone. You opened the door and now I am here. (By the way, your Italian is terrible right now. You really let yourself go.)

Marta One: No. I am not listening to you. It is insane! There is no way I can do this. Jeremy will come to his senses and come home. Life will resume as it was. Everything will be fine.

Marta Two: Get your fucking head out of your ass. You are whipped! What the fuck is wrong with you!? It is embarrassing. I miss US. I miss our curious and adventurous spirit. You need this. WE need this.

Marta One: I am sorry. I just can't. I am not listening to you.

Marta Two: Stop being such a wet blanket waiting, waiting, always WAITING for life to come to you. You want adventure? You want to find yourself again? Start HERE. We are doing this whether you like it or not.

Marta Two basically took over. She researched and planned. She plotted and stashed money away from the tips she was making at her job. She started studying Italian again. She purchased foreign currency for the first time.

She felt a new empowering feeling blossoming in her chest: hope.

Marta One ignored all of this, moving along in silent agony with her life that seemed to be excruciatingly hollow, empty, and inevitable.

Until one day...

Marta Two: I sent a wire transfer.

Marta One: What is that?

Marta Two: A down payment to hold the last spot on that dig in Sicily. I went to the bank and talked to a hefty man in a horrible tie and stained shirt. It was cool. I felt like a spy! This is exciting!

Marta One: WHAT? We can get that money back, right? This doesn't mean we are going.

Marta Two: Oh yes it does. I needed to do something solid so you didn't chicken out.

Marta One: That is only three weeks away! Mom would shit a brick. Omg. I am terrified to fly! We don't even know where we are going. Who we are meeting. Anything!

Marta Two: Suck it up buttercup. We are doing this. We are stronger than you think we are. As for Fran (Mom), don't worry, I'm taking care of that. I have been telling her for months we are leaving to go overseas... She doesn't believe it. So she just... agreed finally because she doesn't believe us. I faked her out!

Marta One: You did? You told her we are going?

Marta Two: Yessssss. Someone has to help us out. This desire to escape from the life we have and rediscover ourselves didn't just appear out of nowhere, and you can't completely blame your heartache. We have wanted to do something like this for a while. I am now in the driver's seat. Just sit back and relax. I got this.

Marta One: Fuck. Fuck fuck fuck.

Marta Two: My sentiments exactly.

The wire transfer went through. Plane tickets were purchased. I (Marta One) continued to ignore it all. I swear to you that I truly didn't believe it would happen. The night before I had to leave, miraculously, everything I needed for a month away was packed into a carry-on. Somehow my connections were planned, and a rented phone appeared at our doorstep.

(Back then you had to rent a phone. It weighed five pounds, cost a small fortune, and was only good for dialing home once a week for three minutes to tell my mother I was still alive.)

I didn't sleep at all the night before my flight. I was scared of everything. Especially seeing my boyfriend before I left. In my desperate attempt to connect, I had arranged to have lunch with him at the New Jersey airport on the way out of town. He had taken that job in customs control, the reason he moved, and happened to be there the day of my departure. Were we still pretending that there was a shred of hope in this relationship? I had hoped so.

The morning of my trip, my mother was in shock. My dad slipped some cash in my back pocket "just in case you need to leave quickly," and I was on my way. I connected in Newark, met Jeremy for lunch, and then boarded my continental flight to Rome where I would have to connect to Catania, Sicily.

I include in the following paragraphs some diary entries from this time.

August 9th, 2004: "It just hit me that I am finally going. Everyone seems to think I am brave at home. I really don't think bravery has anything to do with it. It is more like denial. Just get your flights, make your plans and forget/deny that you are going. By the time that date arrives, you HAVE to go. Hey, you bought the ticket so 'suck it up buttercup.' It is almost as if I am two different people. One that wants tradition... routine. The other wants pure chaos and a chance to explore, to risk the life I know, and to learn about a new one. Why am I even meeting him here? Feels like the last goodbye. I am nervous about the SAIS bus. Will I be able to understand what they are saying? Dov'e al autobus?"

I don't remember the plane ride. I just got drunk to avoid thinking about crashing. Every sound or change in altitude caused my heart rate to spike. I do remember an angel of a man named David Blazen who was a pilot and got me free earphone sets and drink vouchers. He talked me through my fears about flying along the way. I still think of him to this day with a white light and halo around his head. I have met the most amazing humans on my travels, and he is one of them, a pure angel sent to get me through that flight.

The first time my toes touched a different country was at the Rome airport. I made my connection, got my two-tiered bus for a three-hour ride to Licata in the south of Sicily, and then went to an even smaller town called Campobello di Licata. I met a man named Charlie in a rundown cafe parking lot, we rode together in his beaten-up red Renault car, and I soon found myself in an old nursery surrounded by humans who only spoke Italian. This is where I would meet the rest of the people who were to be my family for the next three weeks.

You have to understand that when I arrived, and all throughout my stay, I was the only American most locals had ever seen. They followed me down the street. All the other volunteers were from different countries: Italy, Scotland, Australia, etc. ... and then me, the American. There were about 13 of us. We all shared one room in an old nursery for three weeks together. Bunk beds, open windows, bugs, group meals, small holes in the bathroom floor as toilets.

Diary Entry for the volunteer project: Day One

"Met everyone from the camp. Met new friends Lisa and Sam who are from different parts of Italy; they are the best! The nursery is nice. Small. We sleep in bunk beds and I keep hitting my head in the morning. No air conditioning though. The first night we went to a bar called Manhattans. They love America here, which I find funny. The people are more beautiful than you have ever seen. Life seems tranquil, no worries or cares, slow. The toilets are small at the nursery, I missed a few times haha, and we also have to shower outside!!! There is a house on the hill that I stare at through the window from my bed. Looks abandoned, but it is the most gorgeous thing to wake up to. I wish I lived there. I listen to Nina Simone's "Feeling Good" while looking at it. It makes me feel home. Not home in Pittsburgh, home here."

I loved *every fucking minute of the experience* because I knew it was the opposite of my "normal" life. It was weird and awkward, it had me doing new things and stretching outside of my comfort zone, and that was even before we started digging up tombs from the Byzantine era.

I reveled in it.

Diary Entry: Day Three

"Got up at 7, but I didn't mind. Headed to the survey site. Found hundreds of artifacts dating back to B.C. and prehistoric times. So many cultures have been here, Roman, Arabic, Greek. I found bones from an animal from thousands of years ago and pottery too! My face was so close while digging out a site and a huge spider came out of the dirt in front of my face and scared me. It was huge! Something out of the movies. White, red, and black. Scared the shit out of me. Returned to the nursery early because I had cramps and read my book in the hammock outside. Da Vinci Code is pretty good. It is so beautiful here, a different way of life. Later I am going to the sea with Bianca and Barbara in their car. I have never seen the sea. I don't have a suit so I had to borrow one. Hopefully it fits."

All of these new experiences shifted something within me that I didn't know existed: a hunger to uncover the true person I could become. There is so much I could tell you about that trip. How I shit my pants from eating a candy laxative, how I turned over a stranger's jet ski, got stung by bees, and was coddled by the Italian grandmother of the group with an onion and frozen steak to soothe the sting. How I became known at *The American Death* because I was really great at a game we played, how I went on a date with a Sicilian boy who didn't speak English.

When to listen to my gut. How I discovered relics not seen for thousands of years, dug up by my own hands.

This trip for me was just the beginning of it all. The awakening.

I learned one major lesson there: We *must* push through discomfort to get to ultimate growth and joy. That's it.

Simple, right? No.

We as human beings don't like being in uncomfortable situations. Comfort is easy, it is safe. As I am sitting here typing this, I close my eyes and visualize what my life would be like if I never made this radical step outside of my little world. I try hard, and I can't. I can't see it. I don't want to see it.

Looking back on that trip now, I see clearly that it was the very experience that began to mold me into who I am today. I met my future husband shortly after that trip. Literally, a week later—we didn't know it for several years—but I was in no rush for any relationship. I was in a relationship with myself first now. I had a lot of learning to do, and I was excited to do it.

Traveling also gave me a deep appreciation for the simple life I grew up in, one that allowed boredom to forge my creativity. One that I didn't appreciate until I left and could look back on it with a fresh perspective. One that spawned my love of treasure hunting. My soul craved it deep inside, but I also just loved *doing* it.

I returned home to work for my family company with newly appreciative eyes. I began to travel with every dollar I had and every chance that presented itself. I grew.

There are times I sit in complete gratitude for Marta Two. I thank her for pushing through the discomfort to get to the other side. To know that I needed a radical change to shake my snow globe. The normal life I had planned was no more, and for the first time, I was excited. I took the first steps toward who I wanted to be: fearless, kind, adventurous, culturally diverse, fun, carefree, worldly, open, loved, loving, and most importantly FREE to be the most authentic version of myself.

I knew then I didn't need anyone else to be the best version of me. I had lost myself, but that brokenness kick-started the beautiful process of loving all of me.

Sometimes you need a radical change to rattle your cage and push you from your funk.

Marta Napoleone Mazzoni is an experienced solo traveler and curious creature on a path of exploring the world and herself. Her experience with the tomb excavation in Italy led her on many solo adventures, including helping restore a 10th-century castle in France, sailing off the coast of Ischia to monitor and record whale and dolphin migration and preservation, and restoring homes for the impoverished in Portugal.

Marta is the host of the award-winning podcast "Marta on the Move," which shines light on people's personal journeys and is home to her own stories and lessons she has learned over the years.

After losing her sister Nina to cancer in 2021, Marta created the successful habit-breaking course "3 To Be Me" to help others find balance. She is also a certified yoga instructor and meditation teacher who teaches in schools, at various corporations, and online.

Marta is also a coach and play facilitator, helping others awaken the inner child to find joy and purpose in life. Her play and creativity workshops for events, individuals, and teams, allow others to rediscover their own creativity and confidence, and forge meaningful connections with themselves and others in a disconnected world.

She also offers once-in-a-lifetime adventures through her Marta On The Move Experiences, which feature intimate sailing holidays and retreats overseas and in her hometown of Pittsburgh.

Connect with Marta:

martaonthemovepodcast@gmail.com

www.martaonthemove.com.

From Hell to Happiness: Finding Peace in the Natural World

By Racquelle Pakutz

Have you ever felt like your life is like the movie *Groundhog Day*, waking up with your alarm clock every day to the same old scene? I did.

Here's what a typical morning would be like for me.

I wake up to my dog Jake nudging me with his nose because his internal *feed me* alarm is going off. Eight minutes later, my phone alarm goes off at 5 am... (cue eye-roll). My first reaction is this annoyed voice screaming inside my head: *Why can't you just let me sleep!*

The guilt sets in while I'm dragging my butt out of bed to go feed the dogs; I reason with myself, *they're just dogs, loving animals... stop being annoyed with them!*

I then feel awful as I walk downstairs, reach into the dog food bin, and decide to give them a little extra kibble—as if it's some kind of apology for waking up annoyed. I wait, let them eat, let them outside, wait, then back inside. Then it's back to bed for them and off to get ready for me. Shower, hair, make-up, pack lunch, and it's usually 7:10 by the time I'm running out the door knowing I am once again LATE.

Cue the anxiety. My heart is racing, my throat and chest are tight, and oh my stomach... it feels like there's a critter in there.

But life doesn't stop. Now I'm off to face the traffic...

I find myself driving to work in the morning and simultaneously trying to talk myself into walking into the office. I drive for an hour, as tired as can be, just wishing for a *pause* button in life.

As I drive, I turn on the radio and I start to think about the day... I now feel worse than I did. Oh, I just want to go home, maybe I can call off work? Maybe I'll get into a fender bender and just won't be able to make it today... Then I'd quickly redirect my thoughts: You need this job, your team needs you, you need to keep going and grinding.

It was 2018, and I was only 30 years old. I'd been a logistics professional for over nine years, and I was working my ass off just trying to get ahead in life. I'd given my ALL to this career, and I was tired. I'd put in long days for many years with very few vacations, and when I did take time off, it seemed to always be for a doctor's appointment or a long weekend here or there.

When I accepted my job in 2009, it was a traditional nine-to-five type of office job. However, as the years went by and the company pushed to grow in size, we were required to be at work earlier and stay later to be better than our competition (cue another eye-roll).

We now had to be in the office from 7:45 am to 5:15 pm, and as a manager, I was expected to be there even longer. This was to oversee all the projects and ensure client satisfaction, as my title was strategic client solutions manager. This meant if we had a large project and I needed to get to the bottom of an issue, I'd regularly work until 6:30 or 7, or rarely (but it did happen) 8 pm. That's a 12-hour day with a 65-minute commute there and back! That's getting home at 9 pm, probably getting drive-through on the way... I'm just exhausted thinking of all I did and what I would need to do on the home front afterward.

As these days wore on me, I began to think about other options. I had a business management degree, a substantial length of time in my logistics career, and a proven ability to learn and excel. There was just one GLARING problem... I worked in logistics, a field known for non-compete agreements, which are legally binding documents forbidding an employee from going to another company to do a similar job for a period of two years.

I didn't know if I could even *do* another type of job, as this was all I knew, what I loved, and what I had excelled at. I wondered what else there was for me. Could I do insurance sales like my mother had??? Nope, not my thing.

I knew I loved a good challenge and being given space to use my intellectual abilities to solve problems that actually meant something in this world. I felt that logistics gave me the perfect platform to put my skills to work and really make change happen. (Logistics is the process of coordinating and moving resources—people, materials, inventory, and equipment—from one location to the next. It is an essential field that has recently come to the forefront due to supply chain issues post-COVID.)

Being a small-town country girl, I saw my education and my career path as the way OUT of the small-town feeling of "stuckness." But what I didn't know and had to learn was how to survive in a very competitive, masculine, and money-driven environment. I was constantly being reminded (by my boss) that I was "overpaid" for my position, which kept me in FEAR of losing my job as I knew I had the highest salary and commission structure of my peers because I was DOING that much more.

The thing is that I was just barely covering my bills on a monthly basis, even though, in comparison to my peers back home (in my small town), I was kicking ass at life!

I loved my job, but felt there was something missing. I just wasn't sure what it was. I enjoyed working on a team of young professionals, learning and growing through challenges that came up every day. I loved the communication and how astonishing I thought it was that a small team like ours played such an important role in building the UBS Arena, building the Alaskan pipeline, moving huge machinery across the country, and so many other really cool projects! I just didn't feel like I (the person I thought I wanted to be and the person I was actually being) was in the right place.

Meanwhile, my body was SCREAMING at me for help. I was overweight, the heaviest I'd ever been. I'm a 5'1" small-frame female and was weighing in at almost 200 lbs. I had a negative mindset, I hated my body, and I ignored mirrors, cameras, and my entire body image successfully for many years. That also caused a lot of stress, strain, sickness, and hormone imbalances. I was constantly sad, living in fear of everything in life, anxious about everything and anything, and just *exhausted* every single day.

But my job paid the bills and provided our healthcare. I had student loan debt, credit card debt, medical bills, a mortgage, two auto loans, and all the other expenses of life that I felt all landed on my shoulders. I gave a lot of myself to my job day in and day out, which left very little for me, my dogs, or even my husband at the end of the day.

All of this made me sad. I felt TRAPPED. Trapped in this corporate career that I loved but didn't want to do anymore.

How did I end up here?

Had I wasted almost a decade of my life?

I just wanted to have a career so I could have a family without the constant stress of not having enough money to buy food or feeling unsafe. I knew I needed to break the pattern I grew up in...

Around this time, I began having health issues. I was in constant pain, everything was inflamed, I had daily migraines, and my hips were on fire and shooting pain up and down my spine. I even had a "rebooting," as I now call it, where I passed out after a stressful event, and when I came back to consciousness, I was very disoriented, vomited, and felt faint for quite a while. Now I'd call this my body "fawning" to escape the extreme stress I had built up in my own mind.

I guess I felt unsafe and unsupported, and I didn't even know it yet, but my body clearly did.

This led me to doctors who didn't seem to give any clear answer or direction for how to fix the issues. So I eventually (not quickly) realized I was my only savior. I couldn't continue to expect doctors, practitioners, and other healers to HEAL me when they aren't on the INSIDE. They couldn't see inside my mind to realize that most of my perceived problems weren't physiological but more mentally driven in nature. This realization was a BIG deal. Realizing that the practice of medicine is exactly that, a practice of science and data collection, I turned to other sources for life guidance.

I felt there just *had* to be something else out there to guide me along my way.

This was the first "thought pattern" shift that I had, that really began my transformational journey.

Once realizing that those people in white coats aren't the saviors I had built them up to be in my mind, I then began to search for answers. I went to YouTube and began watching college lectures sharing about the body. I learned about nutrition, stress, psychology, PTSD, and holistic approaches to healing the body. As I learned new things, I found that my thoughts began to shift. I went from focusing on what I didn't want to what I did want and HOW I was going to get there. I began to commit any extra time in my day to learning.

That 65-minute commute was the PERFECT amount of time to listen to an audiobook, podcast, or YouTube clip! Within one month I had consumed over 65 hours of content!

This was a BIG DEAL. I was changing 65 hours of my month to be surrounded by influencers, thought leaders, gurus, college professors, doctors, yogis, etc.

This *completely* changed the way I perceived the world.

I'm not going to lie, this mindset shift was *hard.* Everything I knew was in question. I had NO IDEA what I was searching for, who I wanted to guide me, or what I wanted to ask for. You see, I had a mindset of scarcity, fear, and disempowerment.

Before this mindset shift, I had felt like the weight of the world was on my shoulders.

I started to talk to friends about different subjects I was learning about. This opened many conversations that helped me see that we all have a particular lens or perspective from which we view the world. That the way we see the world is convoluted by the way we experience our individual journeys here on earth.

I said that I came from a small town, but what I didn't share was that I had a rather traumatic childhood—one which now empowers me to be better and inspire others. I now feel a drive to demand change, both internally and externally. I always knew my childhood trauma was my driving force for perfection, and I looked at it as the "healthier way" of dealing with the extreme emotions I held deep inside.

I lived with daily anxiety, alongside digestion and stomach issues, sleep deprivation, and hormonal imbalances. I didn't understand then *how* these symptoms had manifested in my body, but I knew I wanted to feel better NOW.

Thanks to my new way of thinking, I started to put boundaries in place. I would no longer allow myself to work through lunch. I began to walk outside on my lunch breaks, being sure to use my entire 60 minutes to my advantage. The corporate office was in downtown Beaver, Pa., a quaint little town by the river, and I adored taking an hour away each day to listen to a book or podcast, move my body, and take in the sunshine. To be honest with you, THIS was the FIRST time in YEARS I had really SEEN the natural world around me. I'd been living in the hustle and bustle, completely disassociated for the past thirty years of my life! I noticed the birds singing their beautiful songs and the leaves as they changed throughout the seasons, as the LOVE of nature flooded my soul.

This is when HEALTHY HAPPY HIKER was born. I realized hiking made me happy. Being happy made me healthier, and I wanted to be BOTH but just wasn't sure how. I started to hike every chance I got, as I found it was my escape from my work life and my constant ruminating thoughts. I was able to put on my headphones and listen to a lesson or a good book, getting lost in the words as I hiked alone in the beautiful western Pennsylvania woods.

As the months passed, I didn't know it at the time, but I was changing rapidly. I had gained new knowledge of how to become an entrepreneur and how to live a life I had previously only dreamt of. I had surrounded myself with positive influencers through countless hours of audio educational material, and this, in turn, flowed out of me through what I shared on social media.

Those shares then attracted others who related to my struggles. They sometimes reached out to me and joined me on a hike where we could connect, share, and support one another in a safe and loving way.

Support came from everywhere—something I'd never had before.

I started to build a community of men and women who connected with me, supported me, and loved me. This was all foreign to me, as I had a self-limiting belief that life was all about survival, and I was the only one that I could ever rely on. This fundamental core belief had been CRACKED wide open, and it took me time to heal and reframe. Realizing that asking for help is a superpower and being able to be vulnerable, open, and trusting became my lifesaver. I had never really trusted anyone. I had learned through my past experiences that, if you have expectations of others, you'll just get disappointed. I had a mindset that said I am the only one I can rely on. (Again, this was for good reason, as my inner child had to protect myself for survival growing up.)

Realizing that I had years of work ahead of me gave me a goal to focus on, and self-empowerment became my newest obsession.

All the information I was taking in and this new life perspective was moving me forward. I saw progress and felt empowered, supported, and LOVED. I found that my gifts were already here, within me. Through community and connection, I found the strength to overcome the challenge of change and to do it for a better version of myself.

We all have a paradigm from which we view the world, and it takes just one moment to stop and try to view life from a different perspective. Having the insight to view your world through ego-free and nonjudgmental eyes is priceless. It can be the nudge you need to finally take action for yourself.

Throughout the years since my breakthrough, my insight has become clearer as I look back and review parts of my life. In 2018 I was suffering from loneliness, suffocated by keeping all of my traumas inside and pushing them deeper down. Now, as I write this in 2022, I realize that I still have a lot of work to do to release these emotions and allow myself to heal.

The biggest lesson I've learned is that we are always being supported and seen by others even when we don't think we are. Learning how to dig deep and find the inner strength to ask for help can break the pattern and open the doors of infinite opportunity.

Racquelle Pakutz is the president of Zen Freight Solutions Inc., founder of Healthy Happy Hiker, host of Trucker Talks Live, member of the Young Entrepreneur Council, wife, and mother. She began her business journey a few short weeks after graduating with a BA in business management, which she earned over the course of two and a half years. This, of course, was made possible by the fact that she LOVES to learn. This ambition to fill her mind flourished through the opportunities that were in front of her in the logistics field.

After gaining a decade-plus of experience in logistics and learning the ups and downs and rights and wrongs, she chose to leave the corporate world to focus on her health, family, and quality of life. This would mark the start of a new way of life, including healthy living, mindfulness, self-love, and entrepreneurship. She constantly strives to grow and evolve herself and her portfolio every single day.

From books to magnificent future business ventures, stay tuned to her family's journey to learn more about what is possible—and maybe even a little more about yourself!

Connect with Racquelle:

LinkedIn: Racquelle Pakutz

www.linkedin.com/in/racquelle-pakutz-366b666a

Facebook: Healthyhappyhiker

www.stressfreeshipping.us

www.truckertalkslive.com

www.happyhikeracademy.com

From Grief to Purpose

By Maryann Udel

As I look back at the frightened young woman I was over 40 years ago, I never would have imagined that the healing work I do today would be a direct result of the devastating pain I felt when my husband Bob died.

The morning after he was killed in an automobile crash, I was on an early morning flight from Minneapolis, Minn., to Erie, Pa., to plan his funeral. Nothing made sense, and everything felt wrong. The first-class breakfast of scrambled eggs and toast made me cry. Breakfast was Bob's favorite meal.

Luckily, I sat in the window seat and could stare out at the sunrise to hide my steady tears.

After arriving at the Erie airport, my in-laws greeted me with their own sobs and pain. Bob's dad spoke about the things we had to do that day: visit the funeral home; pick out a burial plot, headstone, and casket; write an obituary; pick out the clothes to bury him in and plan the viewing and funeral.

To be honest, a lot of it is a blur. I remember sobbing at Bob's casket and my dad gently guiding me away, keeping his protective arm around me. I remember the friends, acquaintances, and co-workers expressing their condolences and platitudes, which were supposed to comfort me but just made me angry.

It's better that he didn't have to suffer any longer.

He's in a better place.

It's a good thing we didn't have children yet.

At least I'm young and can still find someone else.

I didn't want anyone else! I wanted Bob! Why did this have to happen? I didn't even get to say goodbye!

The days, weeks, and months that followed the funeral dragged on. I stayed with my in-laws because I couldn't bear to be alone in our house without Bob. There were reminders of him everywhere: a letter to me half-typed in the typewriter with some funny photos (him posing with a spittoon) that he wanted to include in the envelope; his favorite plaid flannel shirt and well-worn jeans and boots; the smell of hypo from his photography dark room in the basement; our waterbed (his choice, not mine).

All were pieces of the beginning of our life together that would never be fulfilled.

I did a lot of walking in those days—long walks, because I couldn't stand sitting in the pain and it gave me something to occupy the time. Bob's parents were going through their own pain of losing a son. The three of us were zombies going through the motions of life—wake up, eat, and then try to sleep again. Yet in our trance-like states, we cried and found comfort in our shared, yet unspoken, grief.

After a month, I was ready to make the transition back into my house. My mom came for a couple of weeks (I think) to support me—cooking, cleaning, and just being with me. She helped to ease me into the loneliness of life without Bob.

After Bob's accident, I rarely got into a car, let alone drove one. My mind kept flashing to the image of Bob getting hit head-on while driving on a two-lane Pennsylvania back road; imagining his shock as the oncoming car crashed directly into the driver's side; wondering if he was conscious as the firemen used the jaws of life to open the car door to remove his injured body; hoping that he didn't feel any pain during or after the five hours of surgery to save his life that ultimately failed.

Even though I wasn't in the car or anywhere near the accident, I held that fear of driving. The unpredictable nature of cars and drivers and pothole-covered roads during the long Erie winter kept me walking instead. And besides, the totaled car had been our only vehicle. In my mind, it made no sense to get a replacement one yet.

The plans Bob and I made to eventually live in Minneapolis were gone. Our friends living there had convinced us that there were enough established theatres and TV stations to employ us both. The theatre apprenticeship I had just started there was meant to lay the groundwork for our life in Minnesota until Bob would be able to join me with work as a TV cameraman. All of that ended the day I got on the plane for Bob's funeral.

I wasn't quite sure what I would do next.

My mother-in-law wanted me to stay busy and knew that I had worked as a waitress all through high school and college. She suggested that I apply for a waitress job at a new diner that was a 10-minute walk from my home. It seemed like a doable solution to me. As it turns out, the owner of the restaurant went to her church, and the two of them worked it out that I was basically hired before I even applied for the job.

At the time, I had no idea that this simple job would be the beginning of my turnaround.

I worked the breakfast and lunch shift—6 am opening, Monday through Friday. Easy orders, nice people. The busy pace kept my mind occupied. My co-worker was a career waitress with a following; wherever she worked, people followed. She was full of life, energy, laughs, and joy.

She was also a widow.

Her husband died when she was younger and left her with two children who she managed to raise as a single working mom. She became my guide, my confidante, my protector, and angel. She showed me that it was possible to have a full life as a widow. She showed me by continuing to live, that I could honor Bob's memory.

While I worked at the diner, I still did my regular walks, and most of the time I talked to Bob. I could feel his spirit all around me whenever I went out into the fresh air and moved. On one brisk winter afternoon, I asked him what I should do. I heard him say, "What do you want to do?" Bam! A plan started to develop. There was no reason to stay in Erie. Most of my friends there were couples and only knew me as part of a couple. It was too uncomfortable to be around them.

It was time to utilize my college degree in theatre arts! That's where I felt totally at home. One of my theatre professors in college had guided a few of us through the process of applying for summer theatre jobs before graduation. I knew how to get started and began the search on my own.

Five months later, my home was sold, my car was packed, and I made the drive across Pennsylvania to Madison, New Jersey, to be an apprentice at the NJ Shakespeare Festival. While there, I met people who lived in NYC and got to know the city.

In New York City, I eventually established my life as a single actress pursuing my dream.

You may think this is the end of my story, but it was actually the beginning of the next part of my journey. Life in New York was lonely. My acting classes provided a place for me to get in touch with my feelings and to meet other people. But let me tell you, restarting the dating process was horrible! Under normal circumstances, dating can be difficult. But once a guy found out I was a widow, he'd go running, figuring I was just looking for a replacement. It was also hard for me to get comfortable; I felt like I was being unfaithful to Bob.

I know. Grief really does a number on you. I missed Bob terribly.

After a couple of years, I decided not to worry so much about dating and just focused on my acting career. Acting became my top priority, and I became more comfortable as a single woman. I didn't need a partner to be fulfilled.

Then one day, on my way to an audition, I met Jim. I was going over my monologue as I walked, and it looked like I was talking to myself. When we were both stopped at a corner waiting to cross the street, Jim made a joke— "Talking to yourself is a sign of genius. I should know. I do it all the time." I laughed and kept walking. But he continued to walk with me to my audition. Even though neither one of us was looking for a new relationship at the time, I gave him my phone number before he left.

I booked that job, and two days later Jim and I had a date.

We had a picnic in the park. He made the food and asked me about Bob as we got to know each other; he respected that connection and wanted to learn more; Bob's life and death are a big part of who I am, and he wanted to know everything.

Three years after that date we were married, and three years after that, our son was born.

Over the years, I realized I was the person who always knew what to say in grief situations—talking with my grandmother about death; being the confidante for those experiencing a break-up or someone passing. At work, I was the person people came to see—"Can I talk to you for a minute?"

I could see the evolution of loss throughout my life.

With each challenge that I faced, I reminded myself that if I survived Bob's death, I could get through this too. I know that I would not be who I am now without him dying. I developed more courage, independence, self-discovery, and strength.

Yet, it wasn't until I almost got laid off from a full-time corporate job that I made the decision to become a coach.

As I continued to process my feelings about Bob's death 30 years after the fact, two major moves later (New York to Texas to California), I followed my grief as I learned how to live with it. Feeling my feelings and allowing the tears to flow every time they came opened me to each new step along the way.

This was where I placed my attention when I became a certified life and business coach and founded Sheltering Tree in 2015. I didn't want anyone else to feel lost, alone, or broken in their grief. I focus on helping others find their way through loss. This work is my purpose in life and fully honors Bob's memory.

I chose the name "Sheltering Tree" for two reasons. First, sitting under a big tree has always been comforting and relaxing for me. Second, the tree has deep roots for strength and stability.

I shine a light on what no one wants to talk about, providing hope, help, and permission to feel. I have the privilege of guiding people to a new life beyond their pain. Supporting them to keep going when all they want to do is quit, helping them to find and deepen their strength.

In addition to coaching clients, I regularly speak to educate others about grief.

We *need* to talk about it.

Grief is necessary. It's a normal human experience, and it's important to face it, feel it, and allow it to happen.

Unfortunately, our society doesn't talk about grief much. It's no wonder people don't know what to do, feel like they're doing something wrong, and can't understand why they aren't able to "get over" it already.

There's fear around the topic, and I want to make it OK to discuss.

The initial grief is like being tossed into the middle of a tsunami. You feel like you can't breathe, you get thrown around, unable to find your footing—totally adrift.

Eventually, the storm begins to calm. You get your feet on the ground, but you're still disoriented. All around you, things have changed, and nothing is familiar. You figure out where you are and slowly bring a sense of order back into your life. Yet there's no denying that everything has changed. You must figure out what you can do with what you have now. The next time a storm comes up, you stay grounded when a wave hits.

Loss changes you, but it doesn't own you. There's a misconception that grief goes away, or you hear people asking about how long it will take to get over their feelings. The thing is—you never get over it. Once you understand that there's an evolution to your loss, you can find some peace. The event that happened can't be undone. It's part of who you are now. You learn to live with it.

As I can tell you from personal experience, I still feel melancholy during the month of September because that's the month Bob died. My body doesn't forget, and I've learned to be gentler and don't overextend myself. I am not overcome with grief, but I know that I need to acknowledge whatever I am feeling when it comes up.

There's also the misconception that grief only happens when someone dies. In reality, there are many types of losses to grieve. I have worked with individuals (privately and within companies) who've experienced the death of a loved one, and others come to me struggling with grief from divorce, breakups, illnesses, and job losses. Even changes like retirement, COVID, or an empty nest can leave us grieving.

A few clients had experienced a loss years before we met. For one reason or another, they didn't get the chance to mourn. The feelings were ignored, pushed aside, or buried deep inside. They thought they had moved beyond the pain because it happened such a long time ago. Yet they knew something was still off.

Just because you don't acknowledge a feeling, doesn't mean it goes away. There may be a parfait of unresolved grief layered inside of you. Instead of allowing the painful feelings to flow through you, you might try to dampen the pain with food, drink, drugs, busyness, exercise, or shopping. This may delay the process of feeling but does not make the grief go away. In fact, the feelings continue to grow.

Bottling up emotion is like keeping a lid on a pressure cooker building up steam. Before you remove the lid, you need to release some of it to avoid getting burned. If you let the pressure continue to build up, eventually the pot will explode. Releasing your feelings takes away the pressure.

If it's been years since a loss and you never dealt with it, it might be holding you back without you even realizing it. Stop being brave, putting on a happy face, or pretending you're OK when you're not.

When you tell the truth to yourself (and everyone else), you set yourself free.

If you're dealing with grief, these are the four steps I guide my clients through:

1. Allow—It is important for you to allow whatever feelings you are experiencing to be expressed. This is not the time to "be strong" or to "keep a stiff upper lip." Your feelings may be heightened, and you need to let them out. Write about them in a journal, or talk with a trusted friend, coach, or therapist.
2. Acknowledge—Acknowledge reality. Know what is fact and what might be fiction. Accept that things beyond your control have occurred, and you can't change them. The only thing you can control is your response to the change. Determine how you can live within the reality of the current situation.
3. Adjust—The life you thought you would have has changed. You need to adjust your focus and come up with a new plan based on those changes. Think about what you want to do. Take the time for self-care, and honest reflection, and consider what you *can* do. Then create a plan.
4. Act—Once you have a plan, it is important to also act. Decide what you can do each day, and then make a note of the ways you have helped yourself. Each small step moves you forward in your new life.

Be kind and patient with yourself. Grief is a lifelong journey, and you aren't the only one dealing with it. Get help when you need it.

My own experience with grief taught me that there are no guarantees in life and it's important to appreciate what you have rather than resent what you don't have. There will always be things that happen beyond your control. Accept that and figure out how to ride the wave and live.

I can't change the fact that Bob died. Nevertheless, I can continue to live and grow despite it.

You can do that too.

Maryann Udel was unexpectedly introduced to the world of grief at the age of 24 when her husband died in an automobile accident. Overnight she went from being a young wife to a young widow. Without the assistance of the internet, social media, or formal support groups, she found a way to live, laugh, love, find joy, and thrive.

In 2015, she proudly launched Sheltering Tree to formalize and share the lessons she learned about loss.

Now as a certified life and business coach, experienced in managing individual and corporate loss, she guides individuals and/or businesses through major transitions. Whether it's assisting a business restructure, leading in-person or virtual retreats, her signature Recharge Your Life or Reclaim Your Life Mastermind groups, or working with individuals dealing with the death of a loved one, an illness, a divorce, a break-up, or job loss, she helps people find the ground beneath their feet again, gain clarity, and create a plan to joyfully move forward. She guides them to make peace with the past and live fully in the present, so they can embrace the promise of their future.

Connect with Maryann:

www.yourshelteringtree.com,

maryann@yourshelteringtree.com

LinkedIn: https://www.linkedin.com/in/maryann-udel/

Facebook:
https://www.facebook.com/YourShelteringTree/

Instagram: @yourshelteringtree

Find Your Magic

The authors hope that their stories have inspired you to not only be who you were meant to be but to fight fiercely for your truths, your loves, and your desires.

We all stumble at times, but it's the standing back up and pursuing what lights our souls on fire that makes the difference in our lives and in the world.

May your soul-level magic be ignited and never burn out!

As part of our commitment to positively impacting the world, the authors of Unleashing Your Soul-Level Magic selected Young Adult Survivors United (YASU) to benefit from online sales of this book through Aurora Corialis Publishing. A portion of the royalties collected from these sales will go directly to the nonprofit.

YASU provides a community in western Pennsylvania for young adult cancer survivors and those who support them. Virtual programming is available for those outside of the immediate area. This helps those on their cancer journey to cope and thrive from emotional, social, and financial support with professional guidance. YASU also provides an opportunity for peers to connect with each other as they navigate this part of their story.

If it feels aligned, please support YASU at https://www.yasurvivors.org/.

Facebook: https://www.facebook.com/YAsurvivors/

Instagram: http://instagram.com/yasurvivorsu

Twitter: https://www.twitter.com/yasurvivorsu

Stories Collected by Cori Wamsley

Photo by MEDIA – The Creative Company

Cori Wamsley, CEO of Aurora Corialis Publishing, works with business owners who have a transformational story to share. She helps them easily write and publish a book for their brand that helps them create a legacy and be seen as an expert while building a relationship with the reader.

Cori's process helps them avoid the stress of not knowing what to write, writing for the wrong audience, or telling stories that don't click with the reader, while trying to figure out the whole publishing process and run their business or nonprofit at the same time. She helps her clients get started on the path to a bigger presence, unshakeable confidence in their authority, a streamlined approach to getting their brand in front of ideal clients, and a massive feather in their cap that gets them booked with media and speaking more often.

Cori's bestselling book *The SPARK Method: How to Write a Book for Your Business Fast* and her unique publishing programs empower business owners to get their message heard.

Many of the books that Cori has helped publish benefit nonprofits, including Alina's Light, KindLeigh, The Backpack Program, and Young Adult Survivors United. Cori believes that books are a gift that can give beyond words and is proud to work with authors who want to benefit others with their writing efforts.

In the six years that Cori has owned her own business, she has helped over 150 people become authors, many of whom have published books through Aurora Corialis Publishing, which launched in the spring of 2021 from her early efforts as a book editor and coach.

Cori and her clients have been interviewed for a variety of podcasts, TV shows, and publications, including *Dr. Phil*; *The TODAY Show*; Tampa, Florida News 9; JET 24 (yourerie.com); *The Pittsburgh Post-Gazette*; *The New York Telegraph*; Medium; Thrive Global; and more.

Cori has 18 years' experience as a professional writer and editor, including 10 years with the Departments of Energy and Justice and four years as the executive editor of *Inspiring Lives Magazine*. She also wrote eight fiction books, including the children's book *Monkey Mermaid Magic*, which she coauthored with her daughter London and also illustrated. She contributed chapters to the anthologies *Twenty Won* and *Living Kindly*. Her latest novel, *Braving the Shore*, was published in June of 2022. Cori has been a contributor to multiple publications, including *Brainz Magazine*.

Cori holds a master's and bachelor's in English literature and a bachelor's in biology from West Virginia University. She lives in Pittsburgh, Pa., with her husband and two daughters. When she's not helping others write and publish their books, she's working on her next novel.

Connect with Cori:

www.auroracorialispublishing.com.

Facebook: https://www.facebook.com/cori.smithwamsley/

LinkedIn: https://www.linkedin.com/in/cori-wamsley/

YouTube: https://www.youtube.com/c/coriwamsley

Instagram: https://www.instagram.com/coriwamsley/

Pinterest:
https://www.pinterest.com/auroracorialispublishing/

Printed in the USA
CPSIA information can be obtained
at www.ICGtesting.com
LVHW011225191023
761201LV00008B/197